Hamlyn all-colour paperbacks

I.O. Evans FRGS

Flags

illustrated by Jack Hayes

Hamlyn · London
Sun Books · Melbourne

FOREWORD

This book aims not only at enabling the reader to recognize the more important of the world's flags, but at conveying some of their interest, and revealing the light they throw on the story of mankind. Although many flags are severely practical, denoting a vessel's nationality or conveying a message, flags in general form an essential part of heraldry, which has aptly been described as 'the shorthand of history'.

A few stirring episodes associated with flags are illustrated in the following pages, and if space had allowed many others would have been depicted. In all probability, there is not a country in the world whose story does not inspire its people to regard their flag with pride.

Today, as of old, flags are both practical and emotive, encouraging a sense of loyalty and patriotism. Even someone normally cold to such emblems might well be stirred if, when 'a stranger in a strange land', he saw the flag which recalled his native country. To borrow the words of Dr Johnson in a different context, 'that man is little to be envied' who never in all his life has been moved at the sight of his country's flag.

The descriptions of flags in this book represent the latest information available at the time of going to press.

Published by The Hamlyn Publishing Group Limited
London · New York · Sydney · Toronto
Hamlyn House, Feltham, Middlesex, England
In association with Sun Books Pty Ltd Melbourne

Copyright © The Hamlyn Publishing Group Limited 1970

SBN 600 00123 7
Phototypeset by Filmtype Services, Scarborough
Colour separations by Schwitter Limited, Zurich
Printed in England by Sir Joseph Causton & Sons Limited

CONTENTS

INTRODUCTION

Early flags

Though the origin of flags is unknown, they have never served merely as decoration: their age-old purpose is to symbolize communities and their leaders. The earliest emblems were not flags, but poles tipped with images or other symbols. Such emblems were used in the ancient civilizations of Egypt, Babylon, Assyria, India, and China.

Under the Romans their use became more systematic; the legions bore their familiar eagles and *vexilla,* squares of cloth hanging from a crossbar on a staff and perhaps depicting the reigning emperor.

The coming of Christianity produced new symbols. The Emperor Constantine was inspired by a vision to replace his own portrait on the military standard with the image of Christ or with the sacred monogram formed from the Greek letters *X* and *P, chi* and *rho,* which are the first part of the word 'Christos'; this standard was called a *labarum.*

Other flags, similarly inspired by visions, bore

The *signum,* earliest standard of the Roman army, was used by centurions for rallying troops.

crosses, other religious symbols, or representations of the saints, and these too were taken into battle, especially during the Crusades. Some were flown from tall iron-sheathed masts mounted on four-wheeled frames, so that they could advance with the conquerors in victory, or be rushed into a place of safety in defeat. That used in 1138 at the Battle of the Standard carried the emblems of three English saints.

Flags of various types, displaying their owners' armorial bearings, indicated the presence of persons of rank. These flags formed rallying points in battle, and because to capture such a trophy was regarded as a triumph and to lose it a disgrace, the fighting around them was especially fierce. Indeed for many centuries the fall of an important flag might decide the outcome of an entire battle.

Heraldry

During the Middle Ages the designing of flags became a part of heraldry, which has its own specialized terms and a strict code of rules.

The *vexillum* was the standard of the Roman legionary cavalry, and later of the veteran corps.

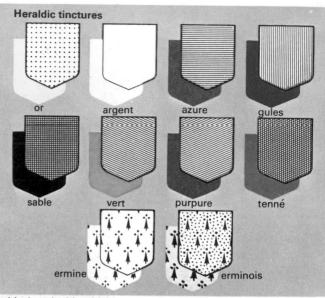

Heraldic tinctures

or   argent   azure   gules

sable   vert   purpure   tenné

ermine   erminois

The black and white shields are symbols or 'hatchings' devised by seventeenth century engravers to indicate colours.

In heraldry, yellow and white are not 'colours': they are 'metals', and are described as *or* (gold) and *argent* (silver). The heraldic colours in Britain are *gules* (red), *azure* (blue), *vert* (green), *sable* (black), and *purpure* (purple). Usage in the rest of Europe adds *tenné* (orange or tawny). There are also several 'furs', notably *ermine* (white with black mottlings) and *vair* (a pattern alternately white and blue).

Heraldry demands that two colours, or metals, never appear side by side; they must be separated by a fimbriation or fringe, a strip of metal between two colours, or vice versa.

Emblems from two flags may be combined by dimidiating or halving them, as in the Cinque Ports flag (page 31). Another method is to quarter them; quartering two, three, and four emblems is shown in the standards of Henry IV, James I, and George I (pages 13 and 15). To symbolize a marriage they may be impaled, placed side by side with the husband's nearer the flagstaff, as in the Queen Mother's standard (page 19).

(Above) arrows indicate the white fimbriation on the Union Jack. Designed according to heraldic principles, the two colours red and blue are separated by a 'metal', *argent. (Right and below)* two of the ways dictated by heraldic usage for combining emblems from different flags. Dimidiating results in the strange lion-cum-herring beast upon the flag of Yarmouth *(right),* and quartering in the state flag of Maryland *(below).*

Becket and toggle *(left)* and the Inglefield clip *(right)*.

Modern flags

Traditionally made of bunting, a woollen cloth woven in Yorkshire in nine-inch widths, flags may now consist of a nylon-woollen mixture manufactured to quite different measurements, but they are still measured by the older usage, a flag of 'eight breadths' being two yards wide.

The ropes to which the flags are sewn end just above the cloth, but a foot or so below it, so that even in a bad light flags are unlikely to be flown upside-down. A toggle or large wooden pin is secured to the rope above the flag and this fastens through a rope loop or becket on the halyards, whereas the rope below the flag ends in a becket which fastens round a toggle on the halyards. In the British Royal Navy Inglefield clips enable flags to be fastened to, or detached from, the halyards very quickly, but to hold quite firmly.

The modern standard is what was formerly called a banner – a rectangular flag symbolizing a monarch or a president and displaying his or her arms. A flag ending in a swallow-tail is normally called a burgee, and one that tapers gently to a point is a pendant or pennant; sometimes, however, these terms are reversed. One tapering more abruptly is simply called a triangular flag.

A country's national flag is that used by its government, and sometimes by its citizens; its merchant flag is that worn by all vessels not in government service. A flag flown at a vessel's stern is her ensign, but as the British ensigns include the Union Flag in the canton – the upper part of the flag in the hoist, the half next to the flagstaff – the term 'ensign' is also applied to a flag of this type. A flag flown on the jackstaff at a vessel's bows is her jack.

Flag usage and etiquette

Because of their symbolism and their associations, flags are treated with respect by all considerate people, and in some countries their use is regulated by a formal flag code. Except

Merchantmen wore the Red Ensign at the stern and a house flag on the mainmast. Today, they may also fly the pilot jack at the bows.

Flag at half-mast to signify mourning *(left)*. Flag brailed, or rolled up and secured with halyards, for 'breaking out' *(right)*.

when for special reasons they fly night and day, they are hoisted in the morning – at 8 am BST in Britain – and lowered at sunset, perhaps with a special ceremony.

A flag may be rolled up and secured with the halyards, so that it can be 'broken out' on reaching the masthead; or it may be hoisted unfurled, either briskly or with impressive slowness; it is always lowered slowly.

One national flag is never flown over another: a sign of conquest in war, this would be regarded as an insult in peace. Flags flown side by side should be at the same level, and as far as possible be of the same size. In front of or above a building, the place of honour is on the right facing the street.

Warships meeting at sea have their own special ceremonial; other vessels exchange salutes by 'dipping' their ensigns, lowering them and then rehoisting them in one movement.

To signify mourning, a flag is first raised to the top of the mast and then at once lowered to the half-mast position, far enough below the masthead to make its meaning clear, and before being finally lowered at sunset it is again raised for a moment masthead high.

To strike a flag by lowering it completely is to surrender. To sail 'under false colours' is to fly the flag of a country to which the vessel does not belong.

A red flag is a sign of danger – or of revolution. A green flag normally means safety, but can give warning of a wreck. A white flag can denote surrender or ask for a truce. A black flag may indicate mourning; adorned with the white skull and crossbones it becomes the fearsome Jolly Roger, the pirate flag.

(Left) pirate flag *(top)*; quarantine flag *(bottom)*. *(Right)* a green flag denotes safety or, as here, warns of a wreck.

GREAT BRITAIN AND NORTHERN IRELAND
British royal standards

For many centuries the English monarchs have flown their royal standards: the Dragon flag of King Harold and the gonfalon of William I are represented on the Bayeux Tapestry, which commemorates the Norman Conquest.

During the Crusades, Richard I of England won fame as Richard the Lion-Heart, and he represented this title by depicting on his arms first one lion, and later three lions, gold on red; this formed the English royal standard until 1340.

In that year Edward III of England claimed also to be the rightful king of France, and he showed that he regarded this as the more important part of his joint realm by quartering the French royal arms, gold lilies strewn on a blue field, with the Lions of England, giving the former precedence by placing them in the first and fourth quarters of his standard.

It remained in use for nearly a century, except that from 1377 to 1399 Richard II impaled this standard with the arms assigned to an earlier English king, Edward the Confessor – five martlets, heraldic birds like martins or swallows without feet, surrounding a cross.

When in 1365 Charles V of France reduced the number of lilies on his standard to three, Henry IV of England made a similar alteration on his own royal standard to show that he claimed not 'France Ancient' but 'France Modern'.

Upon her marriage to Philip of Spain in 1554, Mary I impaled her own arms with his; these quartered the Castle, gold on red, of Castile, with the Lion Rampant, red on white, of Leon (page 121). After her death in 1558 her successor, Elizabeth I, reverted to the Henry IV standard.

Elizabeth's successor, James I of England, was already James VI of Scotland, and in 1603, to represent all his kingdoms upon his standard, he quartered the arms of France and England not only with the emblem of Scotland but also with that of Ireland. The former displayed a lion rampant surrounded by a double tressure or framework enriched at each side and corner with lilies, perhaps to recall Scotland's traditional friendship with France, all red on gold; the latter, devised by Henry VIII, represented a gold harp with silver strings on a blue field or background.

After the execution of Charles I in 1649, the royal standard

(Opposite) the Bayeux Tapestry displays two royal standards: Harold's Dragon flag *(left)* and William's gonfalon *(right)*.

English territorial ambitions in France appear in the standards of Edward III *(above, left)*, Henry IV *(above, right)* and James I *(right)*.

went out of use, and when Oliver Cromwell became Lord Protector in 1653 he flew his own personal standard. This placed his arms, a silver lion on a black shield, at the centre of a flag quartering the red cross on white of England with the white saltire on blue of Scotland and the Irish Harp.

At the Restoration in 1660 no royal standard was available, so Charles II improvized a flag displaying a crown above his initials 'CR', in gold on white, at the centre of the first Union Flag, which is described on page 20.

After James II abdicated in 1689, William III and his wife Mary, who ruled jointly, impaled their arms, but it is not certain whether this device was ever used as a flag. The standard of William was similar to that of James I, except that it bore at its centre a shield displaying the arms of Nassau: a lion rampant, in gold, on a blue field strewn with gold billets or small vertical bars.

Until 1707 Queen Anne used the James I standard. But when England and Scotland, hitherto separate countries ruled by the same monarch, became the United Kingdom of Great Britain, this was symbolized by a new royal standard. The royal emblems of England and Scotland were impaled, with a slight modification, in the first and fourth quarters; the Harp of Ireland remained in the third quarter; but the Lilies of France were relegated to the second quarter, as though the English monarch's claim to the French throne were weakening.

Standard of William and Mary.

Standard of Queen Anne, after 1707.   Standard of George I.

George I, who succeeded Anne in 1714, was Elector of Hanover, and placed its arms in the fourth quarter. They combined those of Brunswick, two lions, gold on red; of Luneberg, a lion rampant, blue on a gold field strewn with red hearts; and of Westphalia, a horse, white on red. At its centre, a shield displayed Charlemagne's Crown, gold on red.

In 1801 Ireland was admitted into the Union, and a year later George III gave up all claim to the French throne. The Lilies of France were removed from his standard; the Lions of England occupied the first and fourth quarters, the Lion Rampant of Scotland the second, and the Harp of Ireland the third; the arms of Hanover appeared on a central shield surmounted by an electoral cap, later replaced by a crown.

Standard of George III.

15

As the Salic law, which precludes female heirs from inheriting a throne, prevailed in Hanover, that country separated from the British Crown at the accession of Queen Victoria in 1837, and its arms were removed from the royal standard.

This now quarters the Lions of England with the Lion Rampant and Tressure of Scotland and the Harp, which now symbolizes only Northern Ireland.

Personal flags of royalty

In 1960 Queen Elizabeth II adopted a new personal flag for use where the British symbolism of the royal standard would be inappropriate. Blue with a gold fringe, it displays in gold the letter 'E', ensigned with the royal crown – having the crown above it – and encircled by a chaplet of roses. It was first used when the Queen visited India in 1961. The same device on a field of the appropriate national arms forms her personal flag on visits to certain Commonwealth countries.

In 1964 the Queen resumed the title of Lord High Admiral, which had lapsed since 1827. The flag of office, an anchor and cable in gold on a red field, is now worn, with the royal standard, by any vessel on which the Queen embarks.

When the Queen is embarked on the royal yacht *Britannia*, the ship wears (bows to stern) the Union Jack, Lord High Admiral's flag, Royal Standard, Union Flag, and White Ensign.

The personal standard of Prince Philip, Duke of Edinburgh, represents his descent from two royal families, the surname he adopted, and his title: it quarters the emblems of Denmark, three lions in blue on a gold field strewn with red hearts; of Greece, a broad white cross on blue; of Mountbatten, two black pallets or vertical bars on white; and of Edinburgh, a black castle upon a rock, also on a white field.

(Left) personal flag of Elizabeth II, used in countries where the symbolism of her royal standard *(right)* would be inappropriate.

Prince Charles's flag for Wales.

As a king's widow, Queen Elizabeth the Queen Mother impales the royal standard with her own arms. These quarter the Lion Rampant of Scotland, all blue on silver, with three longbows on ermine. As her family name is Bowes-Lyon this is a good example of canting or punning heraldry.

Other members of the royal family also have personal standards, the royal standard specially distinguished. The standard of a child of the British Sovereign bears a white 'label' with three points; a grandchild's label has five points. Some labels are distinguished by special emblems. Other members fly the royal standard, ermine-bordered.

The label on the standard of the Queen's eldest son bears no distinguishing emblem, but, as the Prince of Wales, Prince Charles's standard has at its centre a shield bearing the Welsh arms ensigned with a prince's coronet. In 1968 the Queen approved a personal flag for the Prince's visits to Wales; it places on the principality's standard – the traditional arms quartering four lions, two red on gold and two gold on red – a small shield displaying the coronet of the Prince of Wales on a field of green, the Welsh colour.

Princess Margaret's personal standard has a label distinguished by a Tudor rose on the two outer points and a thistle on the central point. That of the Duke of Gloucester, the third son of George V, has a red St George's Cross on the outer points and a red lion on the central point, and that of the Duke of Kent, the grandson of George V, has five points bearing alternately a blue anchor and a red cross.

Personal standard of the Duke of Edinburgh.

Personal standard of the Queen Mother.

Personal standard of the Prince of Wales.

The 'Union Jack'

For centuries the patron saint of England has been St George, and his emblem, a red cross on a white field, has formed the country's national flag.

According to an ancient tradition St Andrew was crucified on a cross formed of two diagonal beams. Some of his relics, it is said, were brought to Scotland, and for this reason a diagonal cross or saltire, white on a blue field, has long formed the Scottish emblem.

When James VI of Scotland became James I of England he wished to represent both countries not only on his royal standard but on a combined national flag which all his subjects were to fly on their ships. Instructed to prepare a suitable emblem, his heralds placed the red St George's Cross, bordered with white, on a field formed by the St Andrew's emblem, to create the first Union Flag. This displeased the Scots, but the King was obdurate; however, he did order that though this new flag was to be worn at the maintop by all British ships,

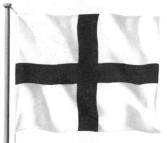

English flag of St George.

Scottish flag of St Andrew.

First Union Flag.

Irish flag of St Patrick.

Since 1801 the Union Flag of the United Kingdom has combined the national emblems of England, Scotland, and Ireland, now Northern Ireland.

one of the older flags should also be worn in the foretop.

After the Restoration, Charles II restricted the use of the Union Flag to royal vessels. In 1674, however, English merchantmen were allowed to fly a Red Ensign with the St George's Cross in the canton, and at the Union of England with Scotland in 1707 this was replaced by a similar ensign with the first Union Flag in the canton.

When, in 1801, Ireland was admitted to the United Kingdom, it had of course to be represented on the Union Flag. The patron saint of that country is St Patrick, and though the emblem chosen, a red saltire on a white field, had nothing to do with him – it comes from the arms of a Welsh family long resident in Ireland – it has become known as 'St Patrick's Cross'. Because the Scottish saltire, as the senior, had to be given precedence, the Irish emblem was placed below it in the hoist and above it in the fly – the outer half of the flag – the saltires being counterchanged or reversed to make the right-hand arms of the red cross higher than the left-hand arms, and vice versa with the white cross.

In this way the present Union Flag was created, the emblem not only of the United Kingdom of Great Britain and Northern Ireland but also of the British Commonwealth of Nations. Though the term 'Union Jack' is incorrect, it is so generally used that to object to it would be pedantic.

White Saltire of St Andrew.

Red Dragon of Wales.

Trinacria of the Isle of Man.

Other national flags

England and Scotland are still represented by the Red Cross of St George and the White Saltire of St Andrew.

The national flag of Wales is a red dragon displayed on a field of white and green, the principality's traditional colours. It commemorates the legend that in a vision Merlin saw a white dragon kill a red dragon which rose again, symbolizing the failure of the Saxons to conquer Wales. In 1953 Elizabeth II granted the flag an 'honourable augmentation', the dragon being surrounded by a scroll bearing the words *Y ddraig goch ddyry cychwyn*, 'The red dragon lends impetus'.

The larger Channel Islands have their own emblems. The flags of the Lieutenant-Governors of Jersey and Guernsey place at the centre of the Union Flag a shield displaying three lions, gold on red; that of Guernsey is distinguished by a sprig of gold leaves. The St George's Cross is hoisted over the official buildings of Alderney; at its centre is a green, gold-bordered circle displaying, in gold, a lion rampant holding a sprig of green leaves. The seigneurial flag flown by the Dame of Sark is also a St George's Cross; two lions, in gold, appear partly in the first quarter and partly in the right arm of the cross.

The island flag of Jersey bears the St Patrick's Cross, a red saltire on white. The state and island flag of Guernsey is a St George's flag, but this may be flown only on land – at sea it is the distinguishing emblem of an admiral of the Royal Navy.

The flag of the Isle of Man bears an ancient emblem said to be of Sicilian origin, the *trinacria*, which represents three armed legs united at the thigh. The national flag of Man places it on a red field, that of the Lieutenant-Governor on the British Union Flag.

The historic symbol of Northern Ireland is the Red Hand of Ulster. It is based upon the legend that a chieftain deliberately severed his right hand and flung it ashore in order to establish his claim to rule the country by being the first in a race to touch it. Placed at the centre of the St George's Cross upon a white, six-pointed star ensigned with the royal crown, it forms the government flag of Northern Ireland, flown also by its citizens. A similar device on a white shield upon a gold circle surrounded by a wreath is placed at the centre of the Union Flag flown by the Governor.

Emblems of the Channel Islands:
(right) Jersey, *(below, left)*
Guernsey, *(below, right)*
Alderney. Placed at the centre
of the Union Flag, the first
two form the flags of the
appropriate Lieutenant-Governor.
The third, centred on the St
George's Cross, is flown over
official buildings in Alderney.

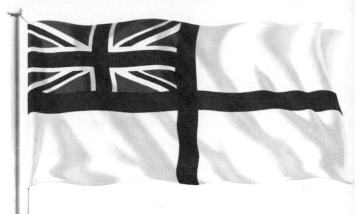

The White Ensign has been the distinctive flag of the British Royal Navy since 1864.

The Royal Navy

For many centuries there was little to distinguish a British ship-of-war from a merchantman, except that a vessel engaged in warlike activities flew from her maintop a very long streamer or pendant. Individual ships were further distinguished by ensigns with the St George's Cross in the canton, the fly being striped in colours chosen by their commanders.

Ensigns of red, white, or blue were later used to distinguish between the three squadrons forming a fleet, the striped ensigns going out of use. In 1707 the St George's Cross in the canton was replaced by the first Union Flag, and in 1801 this was superseded by the modern Union Flag.

The squadronal ensigns proved to be inconvenient and confusing, and during the Napoleonic Wars Nelson gave orders that in the presence of the enemy all vessels under his command should wear the White Ensign; the Union Flag was also to be flown from a foremast stay. These were the colours worn at the Battle of Trafalgar in 1805 when Nelson hoisted his famous signal: 'England expects that every man will do his duty.'. In 1864 the squadronal colours were finally abolished, and the distinctive flag of the Royal Navy – though it is also flown by the Royal Yacht Squadron – became the White Ensign; by this time the flag was no longer plain but bore a large St George's Cross in the fly.

In 1924 George V approved the use by the Royal Navy, for ceremonial guards of honour, of a King's colour. This – now the Queen's colour – consists of the White Ensign charged at its centre with a device including the royal crown and cypher. Following Army practice, the Royal Marines have both a Queen's and a regimental colour. Each bears a device, the former at the centre of the Union Flag and the latter upon the Blue Ensign; this includes a royal cypher ensigned with the royal crown, a terrestrial globe, and the motto *Per Mare, Per Terram*, 'By sea, by land'.

Except when she wears an admiral's or commodore's emblem, a ship of the Royal Navy is distinguished by the commission or masthead pendant, probably a survival of the ship-of-war's long pendant. The paying-off pendant, worn at the end of a vessel's commission, may be very long, depending on the amount of bunting that the signalmen have been able to 'acquire'. The church pendant is flown during divine service.

The badge of the Sea Cadet Corps, placed in the fly of the Blue Ensign, bears the Corps motto 'Ready Aye Ready', and represents a foul anchor, an anchor having a slack cable wound about it, ensigned by a naval crown.

The British Army
Until 1938 the British Army had no distinctive flag, but in that year George VI approved a badge for the Army, placing the royal crest, a lion standing upon a crown, before two crossed swords; on a red field this forms the Army flag.

By custom the masthead pendant *(top)* is lengthened at the end of a ship's commission to form the paying-off pendant *(bottom)*.

The different regiments have always had their own distinctive colours, derived from the heraldic banners of the noblemen who had raised and commanded them. The colours are made of silk and elaborately embroidered, and the colour pike on which they are carried is topped with the royal crest, the lion and the crown, in gilt metal.

As the senior cavalry regiments, the Household Cavalry and the Royal Scots Greys carry rectangular standards. Certain cavalry units carry not standards but guidons – from the French *guide-homme*, 'a guide to the men' – ending in a V-shaped fly with its corners rounded. The light cavalry units no longer carry drum banners swathing their drums; these are now used only by mounted squadrons of the Household Cavalry. Small pennons are attached to the lances used by the cavalry, but these are now carried only on ceremonial parades.

Infantry regiments carry two colours, the Queen's and the regimental. All colours, cavalry and infantry, indicate the actions in which the regiment distinguished itself, by names on scrolls or by special devices, such as a sphinx for Egypt, a dragon for China, and a tiger and elephant for India.

Queen's colour of an infantry regiment.

Nowadays the cavalry carry their lances, bearing small flags called pennons, only on ceremonial occasions. But at the time of the Crimean War pennons were borne on the lances carried into battle, and their purpose as a distinguishing emblem was part decorative, part functional. Here the 17th Lancers, a regiment in Lord Cardigan's Light Brigade, charge the Russian gunners at the Battle of Balaclava.

Royal Air Force ensign.

Standard for an operational squadron of the Royal Air Force.

The Royal Air Force

The Royal Air Force, formed in 1918 by uniting the Royal Naval Air Service and the Royal Flying Corps, represents both in the colours of its ensign. This bears the Union Flag in the canton; its field of 'RAF blue' recalls the colour of the sky, and in its fly are roundels of the national colours, the central red of the Army being separated by a white ring from the Royal Navy's dark blue.

The Royal Air Force colour was approved by George VI in 1947, and resembles the ensign. The square field is fringed in silver and blue, with the royal cypher at the centre.

There are also Queen's colours for certain units of the Royal Air Force; a silver wreath appears within their edges, and their centres bear a distinguishing emblem. That of the Royal Air Force College at Cranwell, for example, displays the figure of Daedalus who, according to Greek mythology, flew with a pair of artificial wings. The colour of the Royal Air Force Regiment, formed during the Second World War to protect the airfields against attack, bears the royal cypher at its centre and displays in its fly an astral or winged crown on two rifles.

The standard for an operational squadron of the Royal Air Force is blue with a surrounding wreath of roses, thistles, shamrocks, and leeks; the squadron badge appears at its centre, and scrolls record battle honours.

Formed in 1925 to identify enemy aircraft, the Royal Observer Corps places its own emblem, instead of the air force roundels, in the fly of the Royal Air Force ensign. Its central device, encircled with a wreath of laurel and surmounted by the royal crown, represents an Elizabethan coast-watcher holding up a torch, and it includes the motto 'Forewarned is Forearmed'.

The badge of the Air Training Corps, an organization formed for the instruction of young men before entry into the Royal Air Force, is similarly placed in the fly of the Royal Air Force ensign; it depicts a soaring falcon and places the Corps motto 'Venture Adventure' below it and an astral crown above.

The badge of the Ocean Weather Ships displays the Royal Air Force Eagle against the sun rising over the sea; this emblem appears not on the Royal Air Force ensign but on the Blue Ensign.

Emblems worn on the RAF ensign:
(above) Royal Observer Corps
(below) Air Training Corps.

(Below) an emblem worn on the Blue Ensign:
Ocean Weather Ships.

A governor-general's flag bears the royal crest with the appropriate country's name on a scroll.

The Queen's representatives

Members of the British Diplomatic Service have their own official emblems. Ambassadors and ministers abroad, ashore or afloat, fly the Union Flag charged at its centre with a white circle displaying the royal arms. Consular officers when on shore also fly the Union Flag, but the central white circle displays a royal crown. When afloat, their flag is the Blue Ensign with the royal arms in the fly, though it is worn not as usual at the stern but at the bows of the vessel which carries them; the Red Ensign may fly at the stern.

A governor or lieutenant-governor of a country within the Commonwealth places the appropriate arms on a white circle surrounded by a garland at the centre of the Union Flag. A similar emblem was formerly used by a governor-general, but this has now been replaced by a blue flag charged with the royal crest and bearing the appropriate Commonwealth country's name on a scroll.

The flag of a Queen's harbour master is the Union Flag, but with a broad white border, and at its centre the royal crown and the letters 'QHM' appear on a white circle.

The lord-lieutenant of a county flies the Union Flag with a central device which places the crown above a gold sword positioned horizontally and pointing towards the fly.

The Cinque Ports comprise several seaports which were once charged with important maritime duties along the south east coast of England. The flag of the Lord Warden of the Cinque Ports – in recent times flown by Sir Winston Churchill and Sir Robert Menzies – is quartered in dark blue and red and yellow, and displays three stylized representations of Dover Castle, a coronet and anchor, a sailing vessel at sea, six composite emblems of a lion and an ancient ship, and a larger representation of Dover Castle.

Trinity House is the principal pilotage authority in the United Kingdom and the general lighthouse authority – with responsibility for over six hundred buoys in England, Wales, the Channel Islands, and Gibraltar. It has several flags, all of which include a St George's Cross in each of whose quarters appears a sailing ship on an 'heraldic sea' of wavy stripes, alternately blue and white.

Lord Warden of the Cinque Ports' flag.

Trinity House jack.

The Red Ensign, flag of the Merchant Navy since 1801.

The pilot jack.

Flag 'H' of the International Code

The Merchant Navy

Except for those vessels which are authorized to fly the Blue Ensign, the distinguishing flag of the Royal Naval Reserve, the emblem of the Merchant Navy is the Red Ensign. As it is better known in foreign waters than the Union Flag, it sometimes appears in foreign flag books as the British national emblem.

Like vessels of the Royal Navy, merchantmen used to fly striped emblems as chosen by their masters. In 1674, as already stated, their flag became the Red Ensign with the St George's Cross in the canton, this being replaced in 1707 by the first of the Union Flags, and this again, in 1801, by the present Union Flag, including St Patrick's Cross.

Though on land the Union Flag is the British national emblem, at sea its use is reserved exclusively for the Royal Navy, whose vessels sometimes fly it on the jackstaff, in the bows of the ship; it is then, and then only, that the flag is correctly described as the 'Union Jack'. Merchantmen may fly on the jackstaff a Union Flag with a broad white border

When hoisted to the masthead the same flag, sometimes

described as the 'pilot jack', is one of the signals used to summon a pilot. Alternatively he may be summoned by hoisting the flags of the International Code of Signals which indicate the letters 'PT' or 'G'.

To announce that a pilot is aboard, a vessel flies either a flag striped horizontally, white above red, or flag 'H' of the code, which is white in the hoist and red in the fly.

To warn intending passengers that she is about to sail, a vessel hoists the well-known 'Blue Peter'. This is the traditional name for flag 'P' of the International Code, a blue flag with a white oblong at its centre.

Displaying, in red, a post-horn ensigned with the royal crown and bearing the words 'Royal Mail' on a white field, the Royal Mail pennant shows that a vessel is carrying mail.

When in port in a foreign country a vessel may fly the flag of that country at her masthead; this 'courtesy flag' is intended to compliment her hosts. The correct emblem for Commonwealth or foreign vessels to use for this purpose in British waters is not the Union Flag but the Red Ensign.

The Blue Ensign, flag of the Royal Naval Reserve.

Flag 'P' or the Blue Peter.

Royal Mail pennant.

One of the earliest house flags, that of the Muscovy, or Russia, Company which was incorporated in 1555.

The custom whereby merchant ships may indicate the shipping lines to which they belong by flying a house flag at the mainmast is of some antiquity, and in modern times it may be supplemented by a special device painted on the funnel.

The house flag of the Peninsular and Oriental Steam Navigation Company combines the colours of the royal houses of Spain, red and yellow, and Portugal, blue and white, in token of assistance rendered to members of both these families by vessels belonging to the line.

Adopted in 1968, the green and white flag of Canadian Pacific Steamships Limited bears a device combining a square to represent stability, a triangle to represent movement, and a circle to represent global activity.

Like that of several other Scottish firms, the house flag of The Clan Line Steamers Limited displays the Lion Rampant of Scotland – though of course without the tressure which would convert it into a royal emblem. The jack of each steamer shows the tartan of the clan after which the vessel is named.

The Cunard Steam-ship Company Limited used to fly below its own house flag, displaying a lion rampant holding a globe, the pennant of the White Star Line, which has been amalgamated with it. The house flag of the Shaw Savill and Albion Company is like the former flag of New Zealand (page 142). That of British Rail symbolizes 'up' and 'down' railway lines.

Shipbuilding companies may also use house flags, which they fly during a newly-constructed vessel's trials. When the vessel's owners are satisfied and take her over, this flag is lowered and their own house flag is raised.

Yacht flags

Vessels belonging to the members of certain yacht clubs are allowed to fly special ensigns. The Royal Yacht Squadron alone may wear the White Ensign; other clubs may use the Blue Ensign, with or without a distinguishing badge, and others the Red Ensign similarly distinguished by a special badge. Apart from these, the flag of British yachts is that of the Merchant Navy, the Red Ensign.

Yachts may also fly a burgee or triangular flag bearing their club's emblem from the top of the mainmast, and a club's flag officer may fly, instead of the burgee, a rectangular or swallow-tailed flag. Some yachtsmen also have their own 'house' flags. Other emblems are used to indicate that a yacht is racing or to denote the prizes she has won.

House flags and funnels of modern shipping lines.

Peninsular and Oriental Steam Navigation Company.

Canadian Pacific Steamships.

The Clan Line Steamers.

Cunard Steam-ship Company.

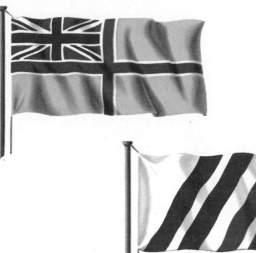

Civil Air ensign.

British Airports Authority flag.

The Civil Air Services

Authorized in 1931, the Civil Air ensign bears the Union Flag in the canton of a flag of RAF blue with a dark blue cross of the St George type bordered in white. It is flown over certain civil airfields and can also be hoisted over air transport buildings and by British aircraft when grounded.

The larger airports, however, are now flying the flag of the British Airports Authority. This is white, and bears four oblique stripes – two red and two purple – which symbolize twin parallel runways.

Although large airports, which are busy at all hours, do not need to display any emblem to show that they are in operation, smaller airfields indicate this by the control tower flag, chequered in red and yellow.

Aircraft whilst in a foreign airfield, like vessels in a foreign harbour, may fly a courtesy flag, that of the country in which the airfield is situated; the appropriate emblem for foreign aircraft grounded in Britain is not the Civil Air ensign but the Union Flag.

The Royal Air Mail pennant, formerly used to denote the

conveyance of mail, has now been superseded by a device painted on the fuselage of the aircraft. It includes the words 'Royal Air Mail' and the traditional crown and post-horn.

The airlines have followed the example of the shipping lines by adopting house flags, flown above the airfields to which their aircraft fly as well as over their own buildings.

The house flag of British European Airways is white and is crossed by a broad red band bearing the corporation's initials; it also displays three astral crowns: crowns embellished with a device of stars and stylized wings.

The flag adopted by the British Overseas Airways Corporation is less ornate but equally effective: a 'speedbird' in gold on a gold-bordered blue burgee.

The only royal emblem to appear on the house flag of a British airline is that displayed by Caledonian Airways; this also depicts a winged lion symbol. The Red Dragon of Wales appears on the flag of Cambrian Airways.

Other house flags are that of British United Airways, which is crossed by two horizontal stripes – in blue and sandstone – and bears black lettering; and that of Autair International Airways, which is blue and displays in white a large letter 'A' and an outlined globe.

British European Airways house flag.

British Overseas Airways Corporation house flag.

Roald Amundsen and his companions, the first men to reach the South Pole, raise the Norwegian national flag on 14 December 1911 to mark the climax of their expedition.

Denmark: national and merchant flag.

Faroe Islands: national and merchant flag.

EUROPE

Scandinavia

Scandinavian flags have a general resemblance to those of Britain, though the vertical arms of the crosses they bear are not placed centrally on the flag, but somewhat nearer the hoist. Ensigns and government flags in Scandinavia have swallow-tails.

The Danish national flag, which is also the merchant flag, is called the *Dannebrog* or 'Strength of Denmark', and is believed to be the oldest of the flags in continuous use.

It resembles the flag of England, but with its colours reversed: a white cross on a red field. The ensign and jack have swallow-tails, and so does the royal standard, which displays the royal arms at the centre of the cross.

Norway was long ruled by Denmark, and later had the same king as Sweden. When, in 1905, its association with Sweden ended, it adopted its own national and merchant flag, which places a blue cross within the white cross of the *Dannebrog*. The ensign and state flag of Norway has three swallow-tails and the jack is square; the royal standard places the royal arms on the ensign.

Iceland: national and merchant flag.

Norway: national and merchant flag.

Though part of Denmark, the Faroe Islands have their own national and merchant flag, which has been in use since 1931: a St George's Cross edged with blue, red on white. Also part of Denmark, Greenland uses that country's flag. Although it has no flag of its own, it is represented on the royal arms of Denmark by a polar bear, white on blue; the Faroes are also represented – by a ram.

Iceland was ruled first by Norway and then by Denmark, and used the Danish flag; step by step, however, it won complete independence, and in 1916 it adopted its own emblem. The national and merchant flag places a red cross fimbriated with white on a blue field, an emblem which recalls the country's colonization by Norway, being the exact reverse of that country's flag. The government flag and ensign is swallow-tailed, as is the President's flag, which bears at its centre the national arms; these include a bull, a vulture, a dragon, and a giant, figures derived from an Icelandic saga.

Of the same pattern as the other Scandinavian emblems, the flag of Sweden is completely different from them in colour, placing a gold cross on a light blue field. It dates from the sixteenth century but was readopted only in 1905 when the union of Sweden and Norway came to an end. The national and merchant flag is rectangular; the ensign, jack, and royal standard have three swallow-tails, the standard bearing the royal arms at the centre of the cross.

The flag of Finland was adopted when the country gained its independence from Russia in 1917. The colours on the flag are light blue and white, arranged in a cross to symbolize the country's waterways and snowfields and to denote its association with the other Scandinavian countries. Its merchant flag bears a light blue cross on a white field; its national flag places its arms on the intersection of the two arms of the cross. The ensign is a swallow-tail of three points, and the President's flag adds an emblem in the canton.

Situated between Sweden and Finland are the Aland Islands. A semi-autonomous part of Finland, in 1954 they adopted a flag which may be flown only on land. This combines emblems derived from its closest neighbours; the field is the light blue of Finland, but it otherwise resembles the Swedish flag, charged with a red cross.

Sweden: national and merchant flag.

Finland: national flag.

Aland Islands: national flag.

Netherlands: national and merchant flag, and ensign.

Netherlands: jack.

Western Europe

The use of a tricolour, a three-colour flag having three stripes, usually indicates that a country has won its freedom as the result of an armed revolution, a purpose for which this simple design is well suited. It would be difficult to produce a complicated flag like the Union Jack or the Stars and Stripes at short notice, or to disguise it without destroying it; but a tricolour can be rapidly stitched together, or unsewn, even more rapidly, to produce three innocuous pieces of cloth.

When in 1579 the people of the Netherlands rose in revolt against their Spanish rulers, they adopted a flag based on the family colours of their leader, the Prince of Orange. It was originally a horizontal tricolour of orange, white, and blue, but the orange stripe was later replaced by red to ensure greater visibility at sea. In this way the present national and merchant flag and ensign of the Netherlands was formed; on days of public rejoicing an orange pendant may be flown above the tricolour. The jack arranges the three colours in a distinctive pattern of twelve triangles, and the royal standard also differs completely from the national flag, bearing a blue cross on an orange field. Another well-known flag is that of the West Frisian Islands, a province of the Netherlands; its field is blue and crossed diagonally by three white stripes on which appear seven leaves in red.

The national flag of Luxembourg was formerly identical with that of the Netherlands, but in 1890 the colour of the lower stripe was changed to light blue. The standard of the Grand Duchess displays her arms, which quarter those of Nassau and Luxembourg, upon an orange field to show her family connection with the royal house of the Netherlands.

During their revolt against Austria in 1787-90, the Belgians chose colours derived from the ancient arms of Brabant. When they won independence from the Netherlands in 1830, these colours formed the national and merchant flag of Belgium, a vertical tricolour of black, yellow, and red. The ensign places the colours as a saltire on a white field, with two crossed cannon ensigned by a crown above the saltire, and a foul anchor below. The arms of the Belgian royal house appear at the centre of the royal standard.

Luxembourg: national flag.

Belgium: ensign.

Belgium: national and merchant flag.

43

One of the earliest French standards displayed three toads, in gold, on a blue field; in AD 496, however, King Clovis was inspired by a vision to convert them into three gold lilies, the heraldic *fleurs-de-lis*. Another early French flag was adapted from the cope of St Martin, Bishop of Tours. Later this was replaced by the oriflamme, whose exact design is uncertain: it may have been blue or red, but it certainly ended in flame-like tongues. What flag St Joan of Arc bore in her struggle against the English is still more uncertain; however, it must have displayed religious emblems as well as the *fleurs-de-lis*.

As already explained, the French royal standard originally displayed a number of gold lilies scattered over a blue field. In 1365, however, Charles V of France reduced their number to three and arranged them in a triangle. On some of the flags they appeared on a white field.

During the French Revolution the Republicans needed a flag, and they had an example to suggest its design – the red, white, and blue tricolour of the Netherlands. This also had the

Legend tells that a vision inspired King Clovis to change the toads on his standard to lilies. Below, an alternative explanation.

advantage that it combined Paris's civic colours, blue and red, with the white emblem of the French monarchy.

The tricolour of France is distinguished from that of the Netherlands by having its stripes placed vertically, blue in the hoist, white, and red. This forms the French national and merchant flag, ensign, and jack, although vessels which served in the Free French Forces during the Second World War wear a blue and white jack, bearing the Cross of Lorraine on a white diamond. Officially the stripes are the same width but in fact they differ slightly, to make them look equal from a distance. The President's flag is normally square, with his initials in gold at the centre.

In 1921 the Irish Free State adopted a vertical tricolour. Though based upon the French tricolour, it combines the green of Erin with the orange of the North, the central white stripe indicating the peace which should prevail between them. Its use was confirmed in 1937 under the articles of the new constitution, and it remained unchanged at the establishment of the Republic of Ireland (Eire) in 1949. The Irish Harp, gold on a green field, which

France: standard of Charles V.

France: national and merchant flag, ensign, and jack.

Eire: national and merchant flag, and ensign.

Germany: North German Confederation flag and later the merchant flag of the German Empire.

had once been the national flag of Ireland, now forms the jack of the republic; the President's flag places the gold harp on a blue field.

Until about a century ago what later became Germany consisted of a number of separate states, and when the North German Confederation was formed in 1867 it united the black and white of Prussia with the red and white of the medieval Hanseatic League to form a tricolour of black, white, and red.

The imperial standard of the German Empire, which was formed in 1871, displayed an eagle, and the naval ensign placed this at the centre of a white flag bearing a black cross, with the black, white, and red tricolour in the canton.

After the First World War Germany became a republic, and the Weimar Convention decided that its federal flag should be striped horizontally, black, red, and gold, but that the merchant flag should be the former black, white, and red tricolour, with the federal flag in the upper hoist.

On attaining power in 1933, the Nazi party rejected the Weimar federal flag, and restored the earlier black, white, and red tricolour. At first with this, and then instead of it, the party used its own emblem: a red flag bearing a black swastika on a white circle at its centre. The swastika is one of the world's most ancient and widespread symbols. It consists of a Greek cross with its arms bent at right-angles, and it was adopted as the symbol of the 'Aryan race'. This flag went completely out of use at the end of the Second World War, being banned by order of the Allies.

After the war Germany was divided into two countries; both adopted the Weimar tricolour. This still remains the national and merchant flag of the West German Federal Republic; ending in swallow-tails, it forms the ensign and jack. The government authorities flag displays on the tricolour a black eagle on a gold shield; this emblem, on a gold, red-bordered square, forms the President's flag.

The East German Democratic Republic also uses the black, red, and gold tricolour, but distinguishes it by the emblem of a hammer and pair of dividers in gold, within a wreath. The state flag places this at the centre of the tricolour, the merchant flag in the upper hoist. The naval ensign bears it at the centre of a red flag crossed horizontally by the national colours, and the Head of State's flag displays it on a red, gold-edged field.

West Germany: national and merchant flag.

East Germany: state flag.

Central Europe

The Swiss flag displays a small Greek cross, white on a red field; the national flag is square, the merchant flag rectangular. Though not a tricolour, the flag of Switzerland recalls the armed uprising against foreign rule by which the Swiss won their freedom. Gautier quotes the chronicler Justinger the Béarnois in explanation: in 1339 they chose as their emblem 'the sign of the Holy Cross . . . for the freeing of their nation was as sacred a cause as the deliverance of the Holy Places' in the Crusades.

The horizontal stripes of red, white, and red on the national and merchant flag of Austria are taken from the arms of the Duke of Bebenberg, who during the twelfth century fought so furiously that his white surcoat was drenched with blood except where his belt covered it.

The national flag of Liechtenstein is halved horizontally, blue over red, with a prince's crown in the upper hoist. The royal flag is similarly divided, gold over red.

The ensign and merchant flag of Hungary is a horizontal tricolour, red, white, and green. The national flag displays at its centre the country's arms, a shield in the same three colours flanked by two ears of corn.

Formerly divided between Germany, Russia, and Austria, Poland regained its national identity, which it still retains, as a result of the First World War. Its national flag is divided horizontally, white over red, and the merchant flag and ensign displays the country's arms in the centre of the white stripe: a white eagle on a red shield. The jack places the arms in the centre of a red-bordered white flag, and on the President's flag the eagle appears on a red field with an ornamental border in red and white.

Also formed as a result of the First World War, Czecho-slovakia unites two former provinces of Austria. Its national and merchant flag combines the white and red of Bohemia, which form two horizontal stripes in the fly, with the blue of Moravia, which appears as a blue triangle in the hoist. The ensign of the armed forces adds in the upper hoist a red five-pointed star on which appears a white lion with a double tail. The President's flag places the national arms on a white field with an ornate red, white, and blue border.

Switzerland:
national flag

Austria: national and
merchant flag.

Liechtenstein: national
flag.

Hungary: national flag.

Poland: national flag.

Czechoslovakia: national
and merchant flag.

Spain: national flag and ensign.

Andorra: one of the national flags.

South-western Europe

The historic colours of Spain are the red and gold of Aragon; though the republic formed in 1931 changed the lower stripe of the Spanish tricolour to purple, the traditional colour of Castile, General Franco reverted to the former arrangement when he came to power in 1939. The merchant flag of Spain places a broad yellow stripe between two narrow horizontal red stripes; the national flag and ensign displays the country's arms towards the hoist. The jack quarters the emblems of Castile, Leon, Aragon, and Navarre. The red flag of the Head of State is crossed by a yellow diagonal stripe, upon which the heads of two 'wolf-dragons' appear, confronting one another.

For so small a country, Andorra, between France and Spain, has a surprising variety of national flags. These combine the colours of both neighbouring countries in a tricolour, blue, yellow, and red, but this may be either vertical or horizontal, and may display either a coronet or a shield bearing the country's arms.

Although the kingdom of Portugal became a republic in 1910 it retained its former arms but altered the national colours. The new government at first wished to put the arms on a red

Portugal: national and merchant flag, and ensign.

Gibraltar: badge on the British Blue Ensign.

flag, but later added green in honour of Henry the Navigator, a fifteenth-century prince active in trading expansion.

The national and merchant flag and ensign of Portugal is green in the hoist and red in the fly. On the dividing line appears an armillary sphere, also in tribute to Henry the Navigator. Upon this a red shield displaying seven gold castles bears a smaller white shield on which appear five blue shields commemorating the victories which the first King of Portugal gained over five Moorish princes in the twelfth century; each shield bears five circles in reference to the five wounds of Christ, in whose name the victories were won. These arms also appear on the green-bordered red jack and on the green field of the President's flag.

To the south of Spain is Gibraltar which was captured by a combined English and Dutch force in 1704, ceded to Great Britain in 1713, and is now part of the British Commonwealth. Its badge, which appears on the British Blue Ensign, symbolizes its strategic value as a fortress and as 'the key to the Mediterranean'; the Latin motto means 'The symbol of Mount Calpe' – the classical name of the Rock of Gibraltar.

Italy: national flag.

Monaco: national flag.

South-central Europe

The modern state of Italy was unified in 1861 when Victor Emmanuel became King of Italy; he placed the arms of Savoy, a blue-bordered red shield bearing a white cross, on a flag Napoleon is said to have designed for his Italian legion. When Italy became a republic in 1946, the royal arms were removed, and the national flag became a vertical tricolour of green, white, and red. Though identical with the former merchant flag of Mexico, confusion was unlikely. But Italy's maritime flags had to be distinctive so the ensign and merchant flag bears a shield carrying the arms of the former republics of Venice, Genoa, Amalfi, and Pisa. The jack quarters these arms and the President simply uses the national flag.

The national flag of Monaco is the reverse of that of Poland; it is divided horizontally, red over white. The royal standard places the Prince's arms on a white field.

Since the fourth century San Marino, near Rimini, has been an independent republic; its national flag displays its arms – three towers, each topped by an ostrich feather, representing Mount Titano's three castles – at the centre of its merchant flag, which is halved horizontally, white over blue.

The dispute between Church and State in Italy ceased when, in 1929, Vatican City became completely independent. Its state flag, gold in the hoist and silver in the fly, displays, in gold, silver, and red, the historic papal emblem, the Triple Crown and Crossed Keys.

The island flag of Malta once bore a Maltese cross, but this was replaced by a flag halved vertically, white in the hoist and red in the fly. For over a century, however, the island's national flag was the British Blue Ensign with a shield similarly divided in the fly. When George VI conferred the George Cross on Malta in 1942, that emblem was added in the upper left corner of both island flag and shield.

Malta, GC, became independent within the Commonwealth in 1964, and the former island flag then became its national flag, still displaying the George Cross. In 1965 it also adopted a merchant flag showing a white Maltese cross on a red field. Approved in 1967, the Queen's personal flag for Malta, GC, places Her Majesty's emblem upon the national flag.

San Marino: national flag.

Vatican City: state flag.

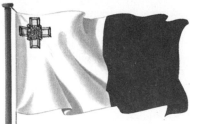

Malta, GC: national flag.

(Above) Yugoslavia: national and merchant flag.

(Right) Albania: national flag.

The Balkan Peninsula

Formed after the First World War by uniting two independent states with regions from the former Austro-Hungarian Empire, Yugoslavia adopted a horizontal tricolour of blue, white, and red, and when it became a federal people's republic in 1946 it added a red gold-edged star in the centre. This is the country's national and merchant flag. The ensign places it in the canton of a red field, but here the star is surrounded by a golden wreath. The jack and fortress flag is red and displays the state arms at its centre: five flaming torches below the red star. This device also appears in the tricolour canton of the red naval ceremonial flag.

Each of the republics forming the Socialist Federal Republic of Yugoslavia has its own flag: three use the same pattern as Yugoslavia itself, with differently arranged stripes, and two are red, one with the national flag in the canton, the other with the gold-edged red star in the upper hoist.

When Albania was freed from Turkish domination in 1912 the emblem it chose was the double-headed eagle, that of its fifteenth-century hero Skanderbeg; this, displayed in black on

Rumania: national and merchant flag.

Bulgaria: national and merchant flag.

a red field and surmounted by a gold-edged red star, forms the national flag. The merchant flag places the star at the centre of a flag striped horizontally, red, black, and red.

Rumania, now a Soviet Socialist republic, became independent in 1878. Its flag was originally a vertical tricolour of blue, yellow, and red. When the country became the Rumanian People's Republic in 1947, its state emblem was added on the central stripe; it depicts an oil-well towering among the trees in a mountain valley with the red star above. This emblem also appears on the ensign, which is white except for a broad blue stripe along its lower edge, and at the centre of the jack, a gold-edged red saltire on a blue field.

The Bulgarian national and merchant flag dates from 1878, the new national arms being added in 1947. It is striped horizontally, white, green, and red. The arms appear in the upper hoist: a lion rampant in gold, with the red star above and a wheel below, flanked by ears of corn. The ensign places a red star on a white field with narrow stripes of green and red along its lower edge. The jack is red and bears a large red white-edged star at its centre.

Greece has two national flags, and these form the basis of several other flags. That flown at sea, which is also the merchant flag, is striped alternately blue and white, its nine stripes being said to represent the number of syllables in the Greek watchword *Eleutheria a thanatos*, 'Liberty or death'; in the square canton a white cross appears on a blue field. A gold crown in the centre of the cross converts this flag into the ensign. The national flag flown on land consists simply of the white cross on the blue field. The square jack and the rectangular fort or service flag add the central crown. A 'target' of blue, white, and blue at the centre forms the civil air ensign, and if the crown is placed in the canton, the air force ensign. With the full arms of Greece at its centre this flag becomes the royal standard.

Cyprus's former badge – two lions, in red, on a white circle – appeared in the fly of the British Blue Ensign. On gaining independence in 1960, Cyprus, still within the British Commonwealth, chose a white flag with a map of the island in gold above two green olive branches.

Against a frieze depicting an umpire and runners in the games of ancient Greece is one of the world's international flags, the flag of the modern Olympic Games (see page 154).
(Right) Greece: merchant flag, and national flag at sea.
(Below, right) Greece: national flag on land.
(Below, left) Cyprus: national and island flag.

(Above) USSR: national and merchant flag.

(Right) USSR: ensign.

Russia and Turkey

When Russia was an empire, its merchant flag was striped horizontally, white, blue, and red. The ensign displayed a blue saltire on a white field, the reverse of the St Andrew's flag. The Czar's imperial standard displayed a double-headed eagle.

The Bolshevist party made use of a traditional revolutionary emblem, the Red flag. When, shortly after the collapse of the Czar's government in 1917, they came to power, it was natural that they should use this emblem, modified by a suitable device, as the flag of Soviet Russia. A British political song, 'The Red Flag', vividly expresses their mood:

> *'It waved above our infant might*
> *When all around seemed dark as night;*
> *It witnessed many a deed and vow,*
> *We shall not change its colour now.'.*

The national and merchant flag of the Union of Soviet Socialist Republics is thus the Red flag, with the state emblem in the upper hoist: a five-pointed star, outlined in gold, above a crossed hammer and sickle, also in gold, symbolizing the workers in industry and agriculture. The ensign of the Soviet Union is white, with a blue stripe along its lower edge, and displays the red star and the hammer and sickle emblem side by side. The jack places the hammer and sickle, in white, at the centre of a red star which is placed upon a larger white star, on a red field.

All the Soviet Socialist republics which constitute the Union have their own flags, most of which place horizontal stripes of various colours across the Russian national flag. That of the Ukraine, for example, has a broad blue stripe.

The national and merchant flag and ensign of Turkey is red, with a white crescent and star displayed in the hoist. In fact Turkey, once part of the great Ottoman Empire, still uses that empire's historic emblem. Legend tells that when Philip of Macedon – father of Alexander the Great – tried by a night attack to reduce Byzantium, later called Constantinople and now Istanbul, he was foiled by the brightness of the crescent moon. Becoming the symbol of the Byzantine Empire, it was later adopted by its Ottoman conquerors; the star is said to be that mentioned in the *Koran*.

USSR: jack.

The flag of a Soviet Socialist republic, the Ukraine.

Turkey: national and merchant flag, and ensign.

Syria: national flag.

Jordan: national flag.

Iraq: national flag.

Bahrein: state or island flag.

ASIA

Western Asia

The Ottoman Empire once included most of the regions around the eastern end of the Mediterranean, and many of these countries still show the Moslem influence either by displaying the crescent moon and star symbol, or by using flags including the colours of the four historic Moslem families: black, white, green, and red, to represent the Abbasids, Omayyads, Fatimids, and Hashemites.

Placed by the League of Nations under a French mandate after the First World War, Syria became a republic in 1941, and though from 1958 to 1961 it was associated with Egypt in forming the United Arab Republic, it never adopted that republic's flag. The Syrian national flag is striped horizontally, green, white, and black, with three red stars on the central white stripe.

The region once known as Transjordan was also freed from Turkish domination as a result of the First World War. The

Kuwait: national flag. Saudi Arabia: national flag.

national flag of what is now the Hashemite Kingdom of the Jordan is striped horizontally, black, white, and green; in the hoist is a red triangle displaying a white star. On a rectangular field of red, green, black, and white stripes, the royal standard places a white rectangle bearing the national flag, with a gold crown instead of the white star.

The region once called Mesopotamia, the land 'between the rivers' Euphrates and Tigris, is now known as Iraq. Soon after the country became a republic in 1958 it adopted a flag striped vertically, black, white, and green, with a golden circle on a large red star at its centre. In 1963 this was superseded by the new national flag of Iraq; this is a horizontal tricolour of red, white, and black, and resembles that of the United Arab Republic, except that there are not two stars but three, in green, on the central stripe.

Bahrein, a group of islands in the Persian Gulf, flies a scarlet state or island flag which has along the hoist a broad white stripe with a zig-zag edge.

The state of Kuwait uses a flag consisting of three horizontal stripes, green, white, and red, with a black trapezium positioned in the hoist.

Though the flags of Saudi Arabia differ completely from those of the other Arab countries, they do not merely indicate but forcibly proclaim their Moslem origin. The national flag is green, bearing in white Arabic characters the declaration: 'There is no god but God, and Mohammed is the Prophet of God'; below this a sword appears, also in white. The merchant flag is triangular in shape, displaying, in white on green, two crossed swords, with a small foul anchor above in the upper angle of the flag.

Yemen: national and merchant flag, and ensign.

Southern Yemen: national flag.

Lebanon: national flag.

The national and merchant flag and ensign of the Yemen is a horizontal tricolour, red, white, and black, with a five-pointed green star at its centre: only the number of stars distinguishes it from the United Arab Republic's flag.

Until recently the region in the south of the Arabian peninsula consisted of a number of Arab sheikdoms, some under the protection of the British, who also had a naval and air base at Aden. However in 1967 the British withdrew, and the whole region became independent as the People's Republic of South Yemen. Its flag is striped horizontally, red, white, and black, with a light blue triangle containing a red star in the hoist.

While under French mandate from the League of Nations, Lebanon flew the tricolour of France with its own emblem, the Cedar Tree, on the central stripe. When in 1944 it became an independent republic it adopted a new national flag, striped horizontally red, white, and red. This retained the traditional 'Cedar of Lebanon' on the central stripe. In the hoist and fly of the jack is a white stripe displaying a red anchor.

When the country then known as Palestine was under British mandate from the League of Nations, its flag was the Blue Ensign with the word 'Palestine' on a white circle in the fly. Renamed Israel, it attained independence in 1948, and placed on its flag its colours, blue and white, and its emblem, the 'Shield of David', which consists of two triangles interlaced to form a star.

The national flag of Israel displays this emblem on a white flag between two horizontal blue stripes; the merchant flag places it in a white oval near the hoist of a blue flag; the ensign also shows it on a blue flag, in a white triangle at the hoist. The President's standard displays on a white-bordered blue flag another religious emblem, the seven-branched candlestick, between two olive branches, and below is the word 'Israel' in Hebrew characters, the whole design being in white.

Israel: national flag.

Israel: merchant flag.

Israel: ensign.

Southern Asia

Most of the flags of Iran (Persia) are unusually long in proportion to their breadth; formerly apple-green, white, and pink, they adopted their present colours in 1933. The national and merchant flag is a horizontal tricolour, now green, white, and red. The ensign and military flag displays upon its centre the national emblem: a lion brandishing a sword in front of the rising sun, beneath a crown and surrounded by a wreath. This emblem, without the crown and wreath, also appears on the flag flown over government buildings.

When Afghanistan became independent in 1919 it retained its former black flag, but in 1929 it adopted the traditional Moslem colours. Its national flag displays a mosque between two sheaves of corn, in white, at the centre of a vertical tricolour, black, red, and green.

The upper and lower portions of the double flag of Nepal

(Opposite) the flags of the United Nations, Great Britain, Nepal and India fly on top of the world at the ascent of Everest in 1953.

Iran: national and merchant flag.

Afghanistan: national flag.

Nepal: national flag.

India: national flag.

Ceylon: national flag.

bear stylized symbols of the crescent moon and the sun.

When the whole Indian sub-continent formed part of the British Empire, vessels of the Royal Indian Marine flew a Blue Ensign bearing the badge of the Star of India in the fly; they also wore a blue-bordered Union Jack at the bows and, when in commission, a red pendant.

In 1947 the sub-continent was divided into two separate areas, both of which remain within the British Commonwealth. The central region retained the name India and adopted a horizontal tricolour, deep saffron, white, and bottle green, with a wheel emblem, in dark blue, at the centre; this emblem, called the *Chakra*, symbolizes the energy of peaceful change. The ensign of the Indian Navy keeps the St George's Cross, to symbolize its association with the other Commonwealth countries, with the national flag in the canton. The merchant flag places the national flag in the canton of a Red Ensign; the Indian Air Force ensign also places it in the canton, but the flag is RAF blue, with a target in the fly formed of concentric circles of saffron, white, and green.

To the west and east of India are West and East Pakistan.

Pakistan: national flag and ensign.

Maldive Islands: national and merchant flag.

The national flag and ensign of the Islamic Republic is tartan green, with a broad white stripe down the hoist, and it displays the Moslem emblem, the Crescent and Star, in white. This flag forms the canton of the red merchant flag and the Pakistani Air Force ensign; the latter is RAF blue, and the target in the fly is green with a white centre.

The former flag of Ceylon was the British Blue Ensign with a badge in the fly depicting an elephant in front of a Buddhist temple. On achieving independence within the Commonwealth in 1948, the island chose as its emblem the Lion flag of the former kings of Kandy. Later the national flag of Ceylon added vertical bars of green and saffron in the hoist. This flag appears in the canton of the ensign, which is white with a St George's Cross, and of the red merchant flag. The earlier Lion flag alone forms the canton of the Sinhalese Air Force ensign; again the fly is RAF blue, but the target, red with a gold centre, bisects two horizontal stripes, saffron above green.

The national and merchant flag of the Maldive Islands displays the Moslem emblem, the Crescent Moon, white on a green rectangle at the centre of a red flag.

67

Malaysia: national flag and jack.

Penang: state flag.

Sabah: state flag.

South-eastern Asia

The Federation of Malaya, formed in 1950 to unite a number of states and settlements, became independent within the Commonwealth in 1957. Having been extended in 1963 to include Sabah and Sarawak, on the north of the adjacent island of Borneo, it was renamed the Federation of Malaysia. Though two years later the island of Singapore withdrew from the Federation, which now consists of only thirteen states, the national flag and jack of Malaysia still bears fourteen red and white stripes, and the star which appears with the crescent moon, gold on blue, in its canton still has fourteen points. The naval ensign places the national flag in the canton of a white flag with a distinctive badge in the fly.

Each of the states which form the Federation has its own flag. The crescent moon appears in gold on the blue canton of the state flag of Malacca, which is halved horizontally, red above white; and in white on that of Selangor, which is quartered red and yellow; on a large red canton in the dark blue flag of Johore; and in the centre of the white-bordered black rectangle which forms that of Trengganu. With its points turned upwards and the star above, the crescent moon appears, with two lances and two swords, all in white on red, on the flag of Kelantan; and in green, with a yellow shield above and wreathed by two coco-nut leaves, on that of Kedah.

Two of the state flags are halved horizontally: that of Pahang white over black and that of Perlis yellow over dark blue. Perak's is striped horizontally, white, yellow, and black.

The state flag of Negri Sembilan is yellow, with a canton halved diagonally, red over black. That of Penang is striped vertically, blue, white, and yellow, with a palm tree depicted on the central stripe.

Of the two states on the island of Borneo, the flag of Sabah is striped horizontally, red, white, yellow, and blue, and in the green canton Mount Kinabalu is silhouetted in brown, while the state flag of Sarawak is based on the arms of an historic figure famous in the region, Rajah Brooke of Sarawak: a crown appears at the centre of a cross halved vertically, black and red, on a yellow field.

The British protected state of Brunei, though also in the north of Borneo, is not part of the Federation. A stripe, divided white above black, crosses its yellow flag diagonally, from the top of the hoist to the bottom of the fly; there is a central emblem of a winged pylon above a crescent facing upwards between two hands, all in red, with a motto signifying 'Always render service through the guidance of God'.

Sarawak: state flag.

Brunei: state flag.

Singapore: national flag.

Though Singapore withdrew from the Federation, it kept its former state flag, which now forms its national flag; this is halved horizontally red over white, with the crescent moon, accompanied by five stars, all in white, near the hoist on the upper stripe. The naval ensign places this emblem in the red canton of a blue flag with a large eight-pointed star in the fly. With the moon facing upwards and surrounded by a circle, all in white on a red field, the same emblem forms the merchant flag of Singapore.

While Burma was within the British Commonwealth its badge, displayed in the fly of the Blue Ensign, depicted a peacock. When in 1948 it left the Commonwealth it based its new flag on the emblem used by the resistance movement during the Japanese occupation. Its national flag is red, with a blue canton on which appears a large white star surrounded by five smaller stars. The ensign places the blue canton with its stars in the canton of a white flag with a large St George's Cross. The merchant flag resembles the national flag except that the whole of its upper half is blue.

Thailand (Siam), 'the country of the white elephant', at one time depicted that creature on a red flag. Annoyed, it is said, on realizing that an ignorant peasant had flown it upside-down, in the 1920s the King declared that he would have a flag whose correct position nobody should mistake; he chose to cross the red flag with two horizontal white stripes, but later a central blue stripe was added. The national and merchant flag of Thailand therefore shows five horizontal stripes, but the ensign depicts the traditional white elephant on a red circle at its centre.

The flag of the Mongolian People's Republic is striped vertically, red, blue, and red; in the hoist an ancient magical emblem, the soyonbo, is shown beneath a gold star.

Burma: national flag.

Thailand: national and merchant flag.

Mongolia: national flag.

Laos: national flag.

Cambodia: national and
merchant flag.

Indo-China, south of China, in the extreme south-east of
Asia, was once ruled by France, and after it had been conquered
by the Japanese during the Second World War, the French
again tried to control that area. The flag of the French Resident
was then a blue burgee, with the tricolour of France in the
canton. In the 1950s, however, what had formerly been
French Indo-China became three independent countries.

The red flag of Laos, independent in 1949, has the national
emblem, a three-headed elephant under a parasol, in white.

The national and merchant flag and ensign of Cambodia,
which attained full independence in 1953, is striped horizontally, a broad red stripe between narrower stripes of blue;
upon the central stripe is a white triple-towered pagoda. This
represents the temple complex of Angkor Wat, probably the
world's largest religious building, which fell into ruins after
the capital Angkor had been attacked by the Chams in 1177.

Vietnam, a region including the former French protectorates
of Annam and Tonkin and the colony of Cochin-China, was the
third country formed from the dissolution of French Indo-
China. But in 1954 the Geneva Convention, in an attempt to

end the war between France and the Vietminh, ordered the withdrawal of forces behind a line of demarcation, and Vietnam has remained divided into two zones ever since.

The flag originally adopted for the whole of Vietnam was yellow or orange, crossed horizontally by three narrow red stripes. It was retained by the southern zone, the Republic of Vietnam. The President's flag is golden-yellow and fringed in gold; at its centre a bamboo tree is depicted in green, and below is a motto signifying 'Duty and Sacrifice'.

In 1955 the northern zone, the Democratic Republic of Vietnam, adopted a red flag with a large gold star at its centre; as elsewhere, the colour and emblem symbolize Communism.

In 1949 the region known as the Dutch East Indies attained independence as the Republic of the United States of Indonesia, and since 1963 it has included Western New Guinea (West Irian). The flag it adopted was that used by the nationalist movement. The national and merchant flag and ensign is divided horizontally, red above white, and the jack is striped horizontally, five red stripes alternating with four white.

South Vietnam: national flag.

North Vietnam: national flag.

Indonesia: national and merchant flag, and ensign.

Communist China: national and merchant flag.

The Far East

China may have been the first country to use flags or banners, and some of these displayed a dragon – which in Chinese mythology is not a fearsome monster but a wise and benevolent counsellor. Some of the dragon flags also bore other emblems, and some had a field crossed with horizontal stripes. When the country became a republic in 1912 it abandoned the dragon emblem but retained the stripes; five in number and coloured red, yellow, blue, white, and black, these represented China's four provinces and its Moslem peoples.

The nationalist government, set up in 1928, of course aimed at ruling the whole country, but it now holds only the island of Taiwan (Formosa); as it hopes to use this as a base for re-conquering the mainland, the nationalist party naturally retains the emblem adopted in 1928. Hence the national flag and ensign of what is still called Nationalist China is red, with a blue canton displaying a twelve-rayed sun in white. The field of the red merchant flag is crossed horizontally by four zig-zag yellow stripes; the jack is similar to the canton of the national flag. The President's flag is red bordered with yellow; the white twelve-rayed sun emblem appears on a dark blue circle at its centre.

The People's Republic of China, which now controls the whole of the mainland, uses the Red flag of Communism. In the upper hoist of the national and merchant flag appears one large gold star; four smaller stars nearby symbolize the co-operation of the republic's four social classes: the town workers, peasants, 'bourgeois', and 'patriotic capitalists'. The red flag of the Liberation Army of the republic places a star and three short bars in the upper hoist.

The island of Hong Kong, off the coast of China, was almost uninhabited until the British occupied it in 1841. Together with a small region on the mainland, it became a crown colony, and is still within the British Commonwealth.

It is represented by a badge on the Blue Ensign, and this formerly displayed a harbour scene, with a junk and a three-masted ship at anchor; on the wharf were shown two Chinese, one apparently greeting a white man is said to have represented a famous native guide.

In 1959, Hong Kong was granted a new coat of arms, which is represented in its entirety in a white circle in the fly of the Blue Ensign in place of the harbour scene. The shield displays a naval crown, gold on red, and below this two junks are shown upon the blue and white stripes which form the heraldic symbol for the sea; the crest depicts a lion holding a pearl, and the supporters are the British Lion and the Chinese Dragon. This badge, surrounded by a wreath at the centre of the British Union Flag, forms the flag of the Governor of Hong Kong.

(Above, left) Nationalist China: national flag and ensign.

(Above, right) Nationalist China: merchant flag.

(Right) Hongkong: badge on the British Blue Ensign.

75

Japan: national and merchant flag, and jack.

Japan: ensign.

The national and merchant flag and jack of Japan, 'the Land of the Rising Sun', represents the country's traditional emblem by a red circle at the centre of a white field. The ensign depicts the sun as emitting sixteen red rays, and places it somewhat nearer the hoist. The Emperor's standard displays another of the country's emblems, a stylized chrysanthemum, in gold on a red field.

Long controlled by Japan, Korea obtained its freedom only when that country was defeated in 1945 at the end of the Second World War, but in 1950 it became the scene of a fierce civil war. In 1953, when the war ended, the region was divided into two separate nations.

The Republic of Southern Korea flies as its national flag a mystical symbol placed at the centre of a white field: a circle half red and half blue representing the complementary principles of Nature. Towards the flag's four corners are black lines whose patterns also have a mystical significance. The ensign and jack places the blue and red circle upon two black anchors in the white canton of a blue flag.

The flag of North Korea, the Democratic People's Republic,

is striped horizontally; its central red stripe, which bears a white circle containing a red star, is separated by a white fimbriation from the narrower blue stripes above and below.

Formerly dominated by Spain, the Philippine Islands won their independence from that country, but passed under the control of the United States in 1898. Though the country was allowed to fly its old revolutionary flag in 1920, this was with the proviso that it should be flown side by side with the Stars and Stripes and that the latter should be given precedence. In 1946 the Philippines obtained complete independence, and the American flag no longer had to be flown.

The national and merchant flag and ensign of the Philippines is halved horizontally, blue over red, with a white triangle in the hoist displaying, in gold, a sun and three stars. The jack also displays the sun and three-star emblem: the sun is displayed at the centre of a blue field, and two of the stars appear in the upper and lower hoist, the third at the centre of the fly. This emblem is based on the arms of Manila, the capital of the Philippines, and dates from 1596.

South Korea: national flag.

North Korea: national flag.

Philippine Islands: national and merchant flag, and ensign.

Mauritania: national flag.

AFRICA

Northern Africa and the UAR

Moslem civilization spread from Arabia across North Africa, and several of the countries in this region, like those of the Middle East, show Moslem influence in their flags; in some by their colours, black, white, green, or red, and in some by the emblem of the crescent moon and star. Later the whole area fell under the control of the peoples of western Europe, and it is only in fairly recent times that these countries have regained their independence.

Mauritania, a region in the extreme west of Africa, between the Spanish Sahara and Senegal, was occupied by the French during the early part of the twentieth century and later became a colony; it then formed part of French West Africa. On becoming independent of France in 1960, the Islamic Republic of Mauritania adopted a green flag displaying at its centre the crescent moon with its horns upturned and the star above, both in gold.

When in 1956 the Kingdom of Morocco became independent it removed from the canton of its flag the small tricolour which showed that it had been a French protectorate. Later in the same year the former Spanish Morocco also gained its independence and was incorporated into the kingdom. Its flags went completely out of use; the merchant flag had been red, with a blue canton edged in white displaying the ancient mystical emblem known as 'Solomon's Seal'. The national and merchant flag of Morocco is now red, and its star takes the form of a green pentagram, another mystical symbol.

The King of Morocco now uses the national flag. As Sultan, before 1956, he had flown a red pendant, bordered in yellow and displaying a yellow 'Solomon's Seal' bordered with green. The green flag of the Caliph of Spanish Morocco, which bore the same emblem, has also gone out of use.

Algeria, which had been annexed by France in 1842 and was regarded legally as neither a colony nor a protectorate but as part of Metropolitan France, won its independence only after fierce fighting, in 1962. Its national flag places the Moslem Crescent and Star, in red, on a field halved vertically, green in the hoist and white in the fly.

Morocco: national and merchant flag.

Algeria: national flag.

Tunisia: national and merchant flag.

Libya: national flag.

Tunisia, which had been a French protectorate since 1881, became independent in 1956. Its national and merchant flag places the crescent moon and star emblem, in red, upon a white circle at the centre of its red flag. Before independence the Bey of Tunisia used a standard of very ornate design. It was striped horizontally, and the central stripe, which was twice as wide as the others, was green and displayed a white two-edged sword; the other eight stripes were alternately yellow and red and bore rowels of spurs alternating with crescent moons, all in colours contrasting with those of the stripes.

Freed from Italian rule by the Second World War, Libya was for a time placed by the United Nations under British and French administration, but the country became independent in 1951. Its national flag is a horizontal tricolour, the central stripe being broader than the others, and the colours of the stripes are said to represent the three regions which constitute the United Kingdom of Libya: red for Fezzan, black with the white crescent and star at its centre for Cyrenaica, and green for Tripolitania.

For centuries Egypt formed part of the Ottoman Empire and was ruled by Turkey. British troops were sent to the country to quell a revolution in 1882, and in 1914 a formal British protectorate was proclaimed over Egypt. This ended in 1922, but Britain and Egypt remained allies during the Second World War. To denote its new status, and its complete break with Turkey, Egypt adopted a new flag, completely different from the Turkish emblem: a green flag instead of red, and three white stars instead of one. In 1953 King Fuad II was deposed and the country became a republic.

In 1958 Egypt, which by this time had become completely independent, formed the United Arab Republic in association with Syria, and though that country soon broke away, Egypt retained the name and flag of the United Arab Republic. Its national and merchant flag is a horizontal tricolour, red, white, and black; two green five-pointed stars still appear on the central stripe. The ensign and jack places two crossed foul anchors in the upper hoist. The air force ensign places the national flag in the same position, and has a target on the fly: a white circle displaying two green stars separates the black centre from the outermost red.

United Arab Republic: national and merchant flag.

Sudan: national flag.

Liberia: national and merchant flag, and ensign.

The Sudan, Liberia, and Ethiopia

These three countries are being discussed separately for historical reasons, each having been in existence considerably longer than the recently-formed emergent African states.

The Sudan had actually formed part of the domains of Egypt from about 2150 BC to 1580 BC, and after periods of precarious independence it was again conquered by Egypt in AD 1801. Later, in 1899, it came under an Anglo-Egyptian condominium, and the flags of both those countries were flown on its official buildings. On becoming an independent republic in 1956 the Sudan adopted its own flag; this is striped horizontally, blue, yellow, and green, representing the Nile, the desert, and the cultivated areas.

Liberia was not formed, so to speak, 'naturally'; it was founded in 1822 by the American Colonization Society as a refuge for the freed Negro slaves of the United States. It acknowledges its indebtedness to America by using a flag plainly derived from the Stars and Stripes. There is only one white star, however, in the small blue canton of the national and merchant flag and ensign of Liberia, and there are eleven

Ethiopia: one of the national and merchant flags.

Ethiopia: obverse of the Emperor's standard.

red and white stripes in the fly to commemorate the number of signatories to the country's declaration of independence.

Ethiopia (Abyssinia) is very ancient indeed; it is referred to in the second chapter of *Genesis* and by Homer, and Herodotus speaks of the 'blameless Ethiopians'. Its flag, which dates only from the end of the last century, may have begun as three coloured pennants. The national and merchant flag of Ethiopia may be a simple horizontal tricolour of green, yellow, and red, or it may bear the national emblem at its centre: the 'Lion of Judah', crowned and bearing a cross. The ensign is blue, with the national flag in the canton.

The imperial standard of the Emperor of Ethiopia resembles the national flag but is fringed with gold and bears a special emblem, the Grand Cordon of the Seal of Solomon. This emblem surrounds devices and is surmounted by mottoes which differ on the flag's two sides. On the obverse it surrounds the 'Lion of Judah' emblem, and the motto signifies 'Conquering Lion of the Tribe of Judah'; on the reverse it encircles an illustration of St George slaying the dragon, and the motto could be translated 'Strong Star of Honour'.

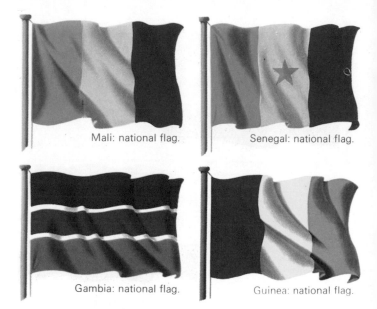

Mali: national flag.

Senegal: national flag.

Gambia: national flag.

Guinea: national flag.

Western Africa

The 'winds of change' which Harold Macmillan, the British statesman, described as blowing through Africa swept many of its countries free of European rule and made them independent – though some remain in the British Commonwealth, and others recall in their flags a former association with France.

Two adjoining countries – Mali, formerly the French Sudan, and Senegal, formerly part of French West Africa – show by the similarity of their flags that they were for a time associated as the Federation of Mali. These are both vertical tricolours, green, yellow, and red, but whereas that of Mali bears no distinguishing emblem – the stylized representation of a Negro dancer having been removed from the yellow stripe – that of Senegal displays a green five-pointed star at its centre. Both became independent in 1960, and Senegal is still a member of the French Community.

Gambia was represented on the British Blue Ensign by a badge depicting an elephant in front of a palm tree, but on attaining independence within the Commonwealth in 1965 it adopted a flag striped horizontally red, blue, and dark green, with narrower stripes of white between the colours.

The flag of Guinea is similar to those of Mali and Senegal, except that its colours are reversed: it is striped vertically, red, yellow, and green. This country was also part of French West Africa, but gained its independence in 1958.

Sierra Leone was founded late in the eighteenth century to secure a home for freed Negro slaves and homeless Negroes from Britain. On becoming independent within the Commonwealth in 1961, it adopted a flag striped horizontally, green, white, and blue. The Queen's personal flag for Sierra Leone, approved in 1961, places the royal emblem on a field resembling the country's arms: the lion under lighted torches and a mountain range or *sierra* are punning heraldry.

The Ivory Coast, independent of France since 1960, flies a vertical tricolour, orange, white, and green.

Upper Volta retained its old name when it obtained full independence from the French in 1960. Its flag is striped horizontally, black, white, and red.

Sierra Leone: national flag.

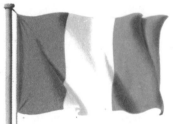
Ivory Coast: national flag.

Upper Volta: national flag.

Ghana: national flag.

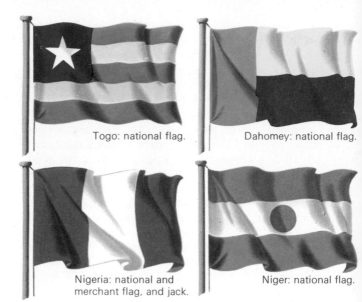

Togo: national flag.

Dahomey: national flag.

Nigeria: national and merchant flag, and jack.

Niger: national flag.

The region formerly known as the Gold Coast was indicated on the British Blue Ensign by a badge similar to that of Gambia, but bearing the letters 'GC' instead of 'G'. In 1957 it became independent within the Commonwealth as Ghana, and adopted as its national flag a horizontal tricolour of red, yellow, and green, with a large black star at its centre.

When the First World War broke out in 1914, the Germans surrendered their colony of Togoland to Britain and France. The British portion became part of what is now Ghana, while the French administered the part adjoining their own colony Dahomey, then within French West Africa. The national flag of the Republic of Togo – its name since this region became independent in 1960 – bears five horizontal stripes, three green and two yellow, and its red canton displays a white star.

Dahomey itself gained full independence in 1960. Its flag has a vertical green stripe in the hoist and two horizontal stripes, yellow over red, in the fly.

The former badge of Nigeria, in the fly of the British Blue Ensign, was a red circle showing the royal crown on a device of interlaced equilateral triangles, in green. Independent in

1960, and a republic within the Commonwealth in 1963, the country has a national and merchant flag and jack striped vertically, green, white, and green; the ensign places the national flag in the canton of a St George's Cross.

Niger, a territory of French West Africa and later for a time a member of the French Community, gained full independence in 1960. Its flag is a horizontal tricolour, orange, white, and green, with a small orange circle at its centre.

Central and Eastern Africa

During the First World War the German colony of Kamerun was conquered by British and French troops, and it was divided later into a British and a French sphere of influence. Part of the British region was united to Nigeria, and the remainder, with the French region, became independent as the Cameroun Republic in 1961. Its flag is striped vertically, green, red, and yellow, with two gold stars in the upper hoist.

The region formerly known as Spanish Guinea became independent in 1958 as Equatorial Guinea. Its flag bears three

Cameroun: national flag.

Chad: national flag.

Central African Republic: national flag.

Congo (Brazzaville): national flag.

horizontal stripes, green, white, and yellow, and has a blue triangle in the hoist; a central shield, in gold, displays a silk-cotton tree and is placed below six gold stars and above a motto in Spanish signifying 'Unity, Peace, Justice'.

What was French Equatorial Africa was divided in 1960 into four independent states, all of which are members of the French Community. The flag of Chad has three vertical stripes, blue, yellow, and red.

That of the Central African Republic is striped horizontally, blue, white, green, and yellow, with a vertical red stripe at its centre and a gold star at the top of the hoist.

The flag of the Republic of Congo or Congo (Brazzaville), formerly the Middle Congo, is green in the upper hoist and red in the lower fly, the two colours being separated by a broad yellow stripe crossing the flag diagonally from the bottom of the hoist to the top of the fly.

The national flag of the Republic of Gabon is a horizontal tricolour of green, yellow, and blue.

The Somali Republic (Somalia) consists of the territories

Red Cross hospitals, vehicles, and helpers bear an emblem symbolizing their purpose: the impartial relief of suffering (see page 154).

Gabon: national flag.

Somalia: national flag.

once known as British Somaliland and Italian Somaliland. The former was represented by a badge in the fly of the British ensigns. It depicted a shield displaying native weapons, a minaret, a dhow at sea, and an anchor; the crest was a kudu's head surmounted by a royal crown. On gaining independence in 1960 the two regions combined, retaining the emblem of Italian Somaliland as their national flag: a white five-pointed star at the centre of a blue field.

The region known as the Congolese Republic or Congo (Kinshasa) became independent in 1960; hitherto the Belgian Congo, it had had its own flag, displaying a gold star on a blue field. In spite of its complete break with Belgium, it still places

Congo (Kinshasa): national flag.

Rwanda: national flag.

Burundi: national flag.

Uganda: national flag.

this emblem on its national flag, but the star now appears in the upper hoist, and the field is crossed diagonally from the bottom of the hoist to the top of the fly by a red stripe which is edged with yellow.

A small area to the east of the former Belgian Congo, Ruanda-Urundi, was originally part of German East Africa, but as a result of the First World War was administered by Belgium, first under a mandate from the League of Nations and later as a United Nations trust territory. In 1962 Rwanda became an independent republic. Its national flag is a vertical tricolour, red, yellow, and green, with a large letter 'R' in black on the central stripe.

That of the Republic of Burundi, also independent since 1962, bears a white saltire with red above and below the centre and green in the hoist and fly; on a central white circle are three green-bordered, red six-pointed stars.

A number of regions in central and southern Africa are independent within the Commonwealth; most were formerly represented by badges on the British Blue Ensign but now have their own national flags.

When Uganda became independent in 1962 it retained its badge, displaying a crested crane, but centred this on a flag striped horizontally in black, yellow, and red.

On gaining its independence in 1963, Kenya abandoned its former badge of a lion rampant and adopted a flag striped horizontally black, red, and green, with narrow white stripes between these colours; an African shield upon two crossed assegais, or native spears, is depicted at its centre.

The German colony of Tanganyika became a British mandate after the First World War, and was symbolized by the head of a giraffe. The flag of Zanzibar was red, but the British Resident placed on the ensign a badge showing an Arab dhow. Both symbolized their independence by adopting new flags. In 1964 they joined to form the United Republic of Tanzania. Their national flag is green in the upper hoist and blue in the lower fly, and is crossed diagonally from the base of the hoist to the top of the fly by a black stripe which is edged with gold.

In 1953 three regions within the Commonwealth united to form the Federation of

Kenya: national flag.

Tanzania: national flag.

Malawi: national flag.

Zambia: national flag.

Rhodesia and Nyasaland, represented by a badge displaying symbols taken from their respective arms. Ten years later, however, the Federation dissolved, its members still remaining within the British Commonwealth.

The former Nyasaland, now renamed Malawi, uses a flag striped horizontally, black bearing a rising sun emblem in red, red, and green. Zambia, formerly Northern Rhodesia, flies a green flag; in the upper part of the fly an eagle appears, and in the lower part are three vertical stripes, red, black, and orange.

Southern Rhodesia then became Rhodesia and flew a British ensign – its blue field lighter than usual – with a badge showing a miner's pick below a red lion between two thistles. In 1968 Rhodesia adopted a new flag striped vertically, green, white, and green. At its centre appear the national arms: the shield displays the emblems which appeared on the British ensign; the supporters are sable antelopes, and the crest, in gold, is one of the Zimbabwe birds, soapstone figurines discovered in the ruined city of Zimbabwe. The motto might be translated 'May it be worthy of the name'.

Rhodesia: national flag.

Malagasy: national flag.

Botswana: national flag.

Lesotho: national flag.

Some African islands

Madagascar was under French rule but became independent as the Malagasy Republic in 1960, while remaining within the French Community; its flag has a broad white stripe in the hoist and two stripes, red above green, in the fly.

Some smaller African islands, being within the Commonwealth, are represented by badges on the Blue Ensign; that of St Helena shows an Indiaman about to sail between two cliffs, that of the Seychelles a beach scene. Mauritius formerly used its arms as a badge but since independence has flown a new flag striped horizontally, red, blue, yellow, and green.

Three states in Southern Africa

Three states in the southern part of Africa now have new flags: Botswana (formerly Bechuanaland), a blue flag crossed horizontally by a black stripe edged with white; Lesotho (formerly Basutoland), a blue flag with vertical stripes of green and red

Mauritius: badge on the British Blue Ensign, replaced by a flag.

Seychelles: badge on the British Blue Ensign.

St Helena: badge on the British Blue Ensign.

in the hoist and with a native hat depicted in the fly; and finally Swaziland, a flag on which two horizontal blue stripes are separated by a broader red stripe edged with yellow and displaying, in black and white, an African shield and spears.

The Republic of South Africa

Cape Colony was settled by the British and by the *Boers* (farmers) from Holland, but friction between the two races induced the latter to set out in 1835-6 on their Great Trek to found Natal, the Orange Free State, and the Transvaal.

In 1839 they founded the Republic Natalia; until this became British in 1843 it flew an adapted Dutch flag in which the central stripe became a white triangle extending from the fly to the midpoint of the hoist. William III of Holland designed a flag for the Orange Free State to symbolize the relationship between the two countries; its white field was crossed horizontally by three orange stripes and it bore the Dutch flag in the canton. The Transvaal adopted the *vierkleur* (four colours) flag, consisting of the Dutch tricolour of red, white, and blue, with a broad green stripe, to represent 'Young Holland', extending down the hoist.

After the Boer War of 1899-1902 the four regions were united as South Africa, and their emblems combined in a badge on the Red and Blue Ensigns: a white-robed female figure grasping an anchor for the Cape of Good Hope; two wild oxen for Natal; an orange tree for what was now the Orange River Colony; and a trek waggon to represent the Transvaal.

When in 1926 the Union of South Africa gained dominion status, it adopted a new national flag, retaining this when it withdrew from the Commonwealth to become a republic in 1961. The national flag of the Republic of South Africa is a horizontal tricolour, orange, white, and blue, with three small flags displayed on the central stripe: the British Union Jack, the old Orange Free State flag, and the old *vierkleur* or four-colour flag. This is also the merchant flag and the jack; the ensign places it in the canton of a white flag with a broad green cross. The ensign of the South African Air Force is light blue with a badge in the fly superimposing a leaping springbok on a stylized plan of the historic fort at Cape Town; the canton is the national flag.

National and merchant flag, and jack of
South Africa.

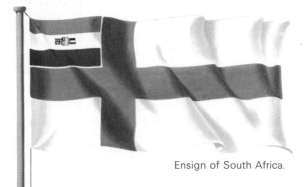

Ensign of South Africa.

Air Force ensign of South Africa.

(Above) national and merchant flag, ensign, and jack of Canada.

(Right) present national arms of Canada.

NORTH AMERICA

Canada

Canada was the first overseas region of what was then the British Empire to be granted its own flag, in 1869. It was the Red Ensign displaying a shield in the fly which quartered the arms of Canada's first four provinces: Ontario, Quebec, Nova Scotia, and New Brunswick. In 1921 the shield was replaced by another, of simpler but more effective pattern, bearing the arms of Canada itself; these combine the Lion of England, the Lion Rampant of Scotland, the Harp of Ireland, and the Lilies of France with the Canadian Maple Leaf.

In 1965 this ensign was superseded by a new national flag, which is also the merchant flag, ensign, and jack. The Canadian emblem, the Maple Leaf, is displayed at its centre, red on white, and there are broad red stripes down the hoist and fly.

A Queen's personal flag for Canada had already been approved in 1961; it centres the royal emblem on a flag displaying the arms of Canada, which are similar to those formerly shown on the Red Ensign. Its upper part resembles the royal standard, except that the English Lions in the fourth quarter are replaced by the French *Fleurs-de-lis*, and below are three maple leaves, red on white.

Approved in 1967, the flag of the Canadian armed forces places the national flag in the canton of a white flag, with the emblem of the armed forces in the fly. This includes the royal crown, the crossed swords of the army, the anchor of the navy, and the flying eagle of the air force.

Since 1955 the Anglican Churches in Canada have had their own flag, a St George's Cross, red on white, with a green maple leaf in each quarter; the arms of the appropriate diocese may be superimposed at the centre of the cross.

Each of the provinces of Canada has its own flag; that of Quebec is older than the first of the Canadian flags.

The French-speaking inhabitants of Quebec have long honoured their *Fleurdelisé* flag, but this became the province's emblem only in 1948. It displays a broad white cross on a sky-blue field, and has a white *fleur-de-lis* in each quarter. The arms of Quebec consist of a shield divided horizontally into three portions. In its upper part appear two *fleurs-de-lis*, blue on gold – later these were altered to three, gold on blue; at the centre a lion, gold on red; and at the base three maple

Queen Elizabeth's personal flag for use in Canada.

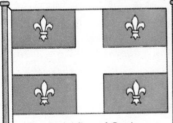

Provincial flag of Quebec.

Provincial flag of Nova Scotia.

Provincial flag of New Brunswick.

Provincial flag of Prince Edward Island.

leaves, green on gold. The shield is ensigned with the imperial crown, and a scroll bears the motto *Je Me Souviens*, which signifies 'I recall'.

The flag of Nova Scotia is based upon the arms which were granted to the province in 1626: a shield displaying the royal emblem of Scotland, the Lion Rampant and Tressure, red on gold, at the centre of a St Andrew's Cross with its colours reversed, a blue saltire on white. This well symbolizes the name of the province, which means 'New Scotland'.

Two provincial flags, both based on the badges formerly flown on the British ensign, display on the upper part of their fields the Lion of England, gold on red, as on the British royal standard. Below, that of New Brunswick bears a lymphad, an heraldic ship, black on gold, upon the blue and white wavy stripes which indicate the sea. On the lower part of the flag of Prince Edward Island is represented an island, upon which three saplings grow beside a large oak tree. These arms were granted in 1868 and 1905 respectively.

Newfoundland is Britain's oldest colony: Sir Humphrey

Gilbert took possession of the island in 1583. It long enjoyed dominion status, but became the tenth province of Canada in 1949. Instead of a special flag it still retains its former badge, which was approved in 1904; this appears at the centre of the British Union Flag as the emblem of the Lieutenant-Governor. It depicts Mercury, the god of commerce, showing Britannia a fisherman who is offering the produce of the sea; the Latin motto signifies 'I bring you these gifts'.

Two of the provinces fly the British Red Ensign, as formerly did the Dominion of Canada itself, but with the appropriate provincial, instead of the Canadian, shield in the fly.

The shield of the province of Ontario places the Cross of St George, red on white, at its top, with three maple leaves on one stalk below, gold on a green field. This device was originally granted in 1907, but its use upon the Red Ensign was officially approved only in 1965. The shield of Manitoba also displays the St George's Cross, red on white, but above a green field displaying a buffalo on a rock, in natural colours. The arms were granted in 1905.

This badge, placed on the British Union Flag, represents the province of Newfoundland.

The province of Ontario places its badge *(above)* on the British Red Ensign.

Another provincial badge worn on the British Red Ensign is that of Manitoba.

The provincial arms are on Saskatchewan's centennial banner.

On the blue field of Alberta's
provincial flag is this shield.

Provincial flag of British Columbia.

The centennial banner of Saskatchewan, although it has not
yet received official approval, was first flown in 1965 to
celebrate the Jubilee of the province. Its colours, red, green,
and gold, symbolize the fires that used to sweep the prairies,
the luxuriant vegetation, and the fields of ripening wheat. The
latter is also represented by the sheaf of wheat in the hoist
and by the three stylized wheatsheaves upon the shield in the
fly, below the lion, red on a gold field, which recalls the ties
of the province with Britain; these arms date from 1906.

Alberta also has a provincial banner, but its design is
simpler: upon a royal blue field are placed the arms of the
province, which were granted in 1907. They consist of a shield
on which appears a St George's Cross, red on white, to represent
the ties with Britain, and below, against the blue sky, a range

of snow-covered mountains which symbolize the distant Rockies, and in front of the mountains a line of hills, a prairie, and a cornfield.

The flag of British Columbia, the most westerly province of Canada, places the Union Flag, with a gold crown at its centre, above the heraldic symbols for the sun and sea, to represent the sun setting over the Pacific. It is based on the arms granted to the province in 1906.

Canada has two territories. The provincial flag of the Yukon Territory was approved in 1967, but the arms which it displays were granted in 1956. They appear on the central stripe of a vertical tricolour, forest green, snow white, and lake blue, and consist of a shield whose upper part depicts a St George's Cross, with a circle of *vair* at its centre to symbolize the British fur-traders, while the lower part bears symbols of two snow-covered, gold-bearing mountains separated by the Yukon River. The crest is a malemute dog upon a mound of snow, and on the flag the shield appears above a wreath of fireweed.

In 1969 the North-West Territories adopted a new flag, placing the territories' badge on a white field with a blue bar in the hoist and fly. The badge is a shield crossed near the top by wavy lines, blue on white, symbolizing the North-West Passage through the eternal snows; a diagonal wavy line below represents the 'timber line' between the forests and the tundra, whose respective emblems are gold rectangles on green and the mask of an arctic fox.

Yukon's arms *(below, left)* appear on a tricolour, as do those of the North-West Territories *(below, right)*.

Raven flag of the Vikings.

'Liberty Tree' flag.

The United States of America
Early flags

Though the Raven flag of the Vikings may have been brought to 'Vineland the Good' by the Icelander Lief Ericsson, the first European flags known to have been unfurled over American soil were those displayed by Columbus in 1492. But as he landed in the West Indies, these will be described later.

Other European flags flew for a time over the French colonies, Quebec and Louisiana; over the Swedish settlements, on the Delaware; and over the New Netherlands, on the Hudson. The British settlers in America also flew the emblems of their homeland. Among these was of course the contemporary Red Ensign, with the first Union Flag, combining the emblems of England and Scotland, in the canton.

Some of the colonies had their own flags: the Beaver flag of New York symbolized the fur trade, while the Rattlesnake flag of South Carolina showed American defiance of British control. The rigid Puritans of New England, disliking the use of a cross upon a flag, devised their own emblems, some of which also suggest a distrust of British rule. The 'Liberty Tree' flag, a symbol of self-government, might bear the words 'An appeal to Heaven', or 'An appeal to God'.

At the Battle of Concord, which opened the War of Independence in 1775, the Americans are believed to have carried a flag very similar to the Parliamentary cavalry standard of the British Civil War: an arm emerging from a cloud and grasping a sword, with a Latin watchword meaning 'Conquer or die'.

Well known in American waters was the flag of the British East India Company; with the first Union Flag in the canton it bore from nine to thirteen red and white horizontal stripes in its fly. Whether the flag which the Americans first raised at Cambridge, Massachusetts, on 1 January 1776 was actually based on that of the East India Company is uncertain, but the resemblance is striking. It could have been devised independently, however, by placing six white stripes on the Red Ensign. In this Union flag, also called the 'Congress flag', the thirteen stripes represented the thirteen states of the Union, while the British emblem in the canton showed reluctance to break completely with the mother country.

Battle of Concord flag.

Rattlesnake flag of South Carolina.

Congress flag, Cambridge 1776.

The Union flag of 1777 *(above, left)* had thirteen stars and stripes. Eighteen years later, two more states joined the Union — hence the Union flag of 1795 *(above, right)*. The Rattlesnake jack *(left)* is said to have been worn by 'vessels of war'.

DON'T TREAD ON ME

But a break was inevitable, and on 4 July 1776 came the Declaration of Independence. It was clear that as the canton of the Congress flag symbolized a now hostile country the Americans needed a new emblem. So, on 14 June 1777, Congress 'Resolved that the flag of the United States be thirteen stripes alternate red and white, that the Union be thirteen stars white in a blue field, representing a new constellation.'.

As the exact arrangement of the stripes and stars was not specified, individual flag-makers used their own judgment, producing several variants. Meanwhile other flags appeared: 'vessels of war' are said to have worn a jack displaying a rattlesnake across thirteen red and white stripes, and merchantmen to have flown a flag with thirteen stripes only.

When two more states were admitted into the Union, the American flag had to be suitably adapted, and Congress enacted that 'from and after 1 May 1795 the flag of the United States be fifteen stripes and the Union be fifteen stars.'. It was this flag which inspired Francis Scott Key, when he saw it flying over Fort McHenry, to write what is now the American national anthem, 'The Star-Spangled Banner'.

Francis Scott Key's moment of
inspiration. Dawn comes, and
the captive attorney, forced by
the British to witness the attack
on Fort McHenry, sees the
American flag still flying over
the fort.

The Stars and Bars, the first Confederate flag.

Confederate battle flag.

Flags of the Confederacy

When, in 1861, eleven of the states seceded from the Union they devised their own emblem. The first Confederate flag, adopted on 5 March 1861, was the Stars and Bars. While retaining the symbols dear to all Americans, it reduced the number of stars to seven, that of the states which first seceded, arranged them in a circle on a blue canton, and displayed on its fly three broad stripes, red, white, and red.

This flag, however, was found to be impractical; its resemblance to the Stars and Stripes might lead to confusion in battle. A more distinctive emblem, though never legally adopted, soon won general approval: 'It was not the flag of the Confederacy, but simply the banner – the battle flag – of the Confederate soldier.'. It displayed thirteen stars upon a blue saltire, edged with white, on a red field.

Though satisfactory on land, the battle flag was ill-suited for naval use, as it could not be reversed to make a distress signal. It was therefore placed in the canton of an ensign with a plain white fly; in case this should be mistaken for a flag of truce, a broad red stripe was later added in the fly.

Modern flags

Meanwhile new stars had been added in the canton of the American flag as new states were admitted into the Union, and so the Stars and Stripes evolved its present form. As the national and merchant flag and ensign of the United States, it now displays fifty stars in the canton – which itself forms the United States jack – while its fly retains the original thirteen stripes.

Whereas in Britain loyalty is centred on the Sovereign, in the United States it is focused upon the flag. To ensure uniformity in its use, a flag code was drawn up in 1923, and in 1942 it was legally established; it has also served as a basis for the similar codes of certain other countries. Two of its more important clauses run:

'The flag should never be used for advertising purposes in any manner whatsoever . . .' and *'The following is designated as the pledge of allegiance to the flag: "I pledge allegiance to the flag of the United States of America and to the Republic for which it stands, one Nation under God, indivisible, with liberty and justice for all."'*.

The Stars and Stripes is the national and merchant flag, and ensign of the United States of America. It bears the thirteen stripes of the first Union flag but the stars in the canton now number fifty to represent the fifty states of the Union.

(Right) United States presidential flag.

(Below) United States yacht ensign.

The President of the United States is empowered to design his own flag, but its field is always blue. As at present in use it displays the presidential seal: this shows the American Eagle grasping in its talons the emblems of peace and war, a number of arrows and an olive branch. Thirteen stars appear around its head and it is surrounded by a circle of fifty stars, symbolizing the original and the present number of states in the Union. A shield of the national colours bearing seven white and six red stripes also appears, and the Latin motto *E Pluribus Unum* signifies 'From Many, One'. The flag of the Vice-President is somewhat similar, but its field is white, and the heads of the various executive departments have their own appropriate flags.

The United States Navy flies the Stars and Stripes as its ensign and its fifty-star canton as its jack. The warship pennant has seven white stars in its blue hoist; the fly is divided horizontally, red over white, and tapers gently to a split point. The 'official unofficial' homeward bound pennant is as long as the accessible material will allow! The church pennant, displaying a blue Latin cross on a white field, is the only flag

The District of Columbia has the same boundaries as Washington, the capital city of the United States which was named after the hero of American independence. Created to give Congress exclusive legislative powers over the seat of government, the District flies a flag *(above)* which derives appropriately from the arms of George Washington *(right)*.

which may ever be flown above the Stars and Stripes, and then only during divine service.

Units of the United States Army have a national and a regimental standard or colour. The standard of the United States Marine Corps displays on a red field the terrestrial globe showing the New World, surmounted by the American Eagle and placed in front of an anchor. The Stars and Stripes forms the colours of the United States Air Force.

United States yachts may be authorized to wear a special ensign whose blue canton displays thirteen stars arranged round a foul anchor. The ensign of the United States Power Squadron has a similar canton except that it is red; the fly contains thirteen blue and white vertical stripes.

The coastguard ensign and Customs Service flag display the eagle in the canton, blue on white, and sixteen vertical red and white stripes, with a suitable badge, in the fly.

The flag of the District of Columbia, in which the American capital, Washington, is situated, derives from the arms of George Washington. It displays three red 'mullets' – the rowels of spurs – above two horizontal stripes, red on white.

Flags of the states

Each of the fifty states in the Union has its own flag, and though some of these emblems simply reproduce the state seal, others are of bold and original design.

The emblem of Alabama recalls in its pattern, though not in its colour, the Confederate battle flag, in which it is thought to have its origin.

The flag of Alaska was chosen in open competition from a design submitted by a schoolboy; it represents the constellation of the Great Bear and the North Star.

Arizona's flag displays the colours of Imperial Spain, by which this region was once ruled, as well as those of the state itself; the coppery 'Arizona Star' is centred on a stylized view of the sun setting over the sea.

The stars on the flag of Arkansas recall the state's history. The three below its name indicate that at different times it has belonged to Spain, France, and the United States; the upper star that it formed part of the Confederacy; and the stars surrounding the central white 'diamond' that it was the twenty-fifth state to be admitted to the Union.

Ruled by Spain and then by Mexico, California at last won independence; the flag it then improvized, displaying a red star and a grizzly bear, was a basis for its present emblem.

The sunshine, the blue skies, and the snowy mountains of Colorado are represented on its flag by the golden disc within the letter 'C' and by the stripes of blue and white.

The three grape-vines upon the shield on the flag of Connecticut recall the three English colonies which united to form this state; the Latin motto *Qui transtulit sustenit* could be translated 'He Who brought us over sustains us'.

The coat of arms on the flag of Delaware includes emblems of trade and agriculture; it shows the date, 'December 7, 1787', on which the state entered the Union.

The red saltire on the flag of Florida also recalls the Confederate battle flag; the central device symbolizes the state's name and the arrival of Western civilization.

The flag of Georgia originally followed the Stars and Bars by having its fly striped horizontally, red, white, and red, but the stripes have been replaced by the Confederate battle flag; the state seal appears in the hoist.

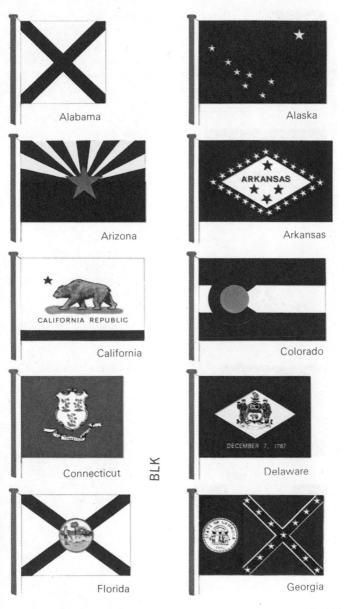

Alabama

Alaska

Arizona

Arkansas

California

Colorado

Connecticut

BLK

Delaware

Florida

Georgia

Hawaii

Idaho

Illinois

Indiana

Iowa

Hawaii, which became the fiftieth state of the Union in 1960, has been ruled by the United States since 1900, but it still keeps its original flag, which shows that it was formerly under British influence.

The supporters on the coat of arms shown on the seal and flag of Idaho symbolize industry and freedom, the wheatsheaf represents agriculture, and the Latin motto *Esto Perpetua* expresses the hope 'May she endure for ever'.

Two national emblems, the American Eagle and a shield bearing the thirteen stars and stripes, appear on the seal and flag of Illinois; the motto reads 'State Sovereignty, National Union'.

After using the Stars and Stripes as its emblem, Indiana adopted its own state flag bearing the traditional symbol of knowledge, a flaming torch; the large star above this represents Indiana itself, the other stars the eighteen states already in the Union when it was admitted.

Purchased by the United States from France, Iowa still flies the French tricolour with its central stripe broadened; here the American Eagle is shown with a scroll bearing the state motto: 'Our liberties we prize and our rights we will maintain'.

The seal shown on the flag of Kansas displays symbols recalling the state's development; above it is the state flower, and the Latin motto *Ad Astra per Aspera* signifies 'Through hardship to the stars'.

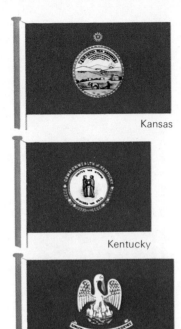
Kansas

The two men depicted on the seal and flag of Kentucky exemplify the motto 'United we stand, divided we fall'; the golden-rod shown is the state flower.

Kentucky

The flag of Louisiana has been used since, and was probably inspired by, the second Anglo-American war; the 'pelican in its piety', nourishing its young with its own blood, is an heraldic symbol for self-sacrifice.

Louisiana

The state coat of arms on the flag of Maine includes the 'Liberty Tree'; the supporters represent agriculture and seamanship, and the North Star symbolizes the Latin motto *Dirigo*, 'I direct'.

Maine

Dating from 1684, Maryland's flag bears the arms of George Calvert, Lord Baltimore, who founded the state by royal charter.

The shields on the obverse and reverse of the flag of Massachusetts respectively depict an Indian and the

Maryland

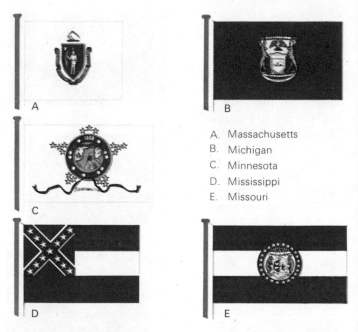

A. Massachusetts
B. Michigan
C. Minnesota
D. Mississippi
E. Missouri

'Liberty Tree'. The motto *Ense Petit Placidam sub Libertate Quietem* signifies 'With the sword she seeks peace in freedom'.

The landscape depicted on the flag of Michigan illustrates the motto *Si Quaeris Peninsulam Amoenam Circumspice*, 'If you seek a pleasant peninsula, look around you'. The word *Tuebor* – 'I will defend' – may recall the Anglo-American wars, for the state is on the Canadian frontier.

The flag of Minnesota is white on the obverse and blue on the reverse, and bears emblems of the retreat of the Red Men and the spread of agriculture; the arrangement of the stars symbolizes the 'North Star State', *L'Etoile du Nord*.

The canton of the flag of Mississippi bears the Confederate battle flag; the three stripes in the fly recall the tricolour of France, from which the state was colonized.

The tricolour of France is also recalled by the flag of Missouri; the Latin motto on the seal *Salus Populi Suprema Lex Esto* means 'The people's welfare is the supreme law'.

The landscape depicted on the seal and flag of Montana

includes the symbols of agriculture and mining, the latter also being referred to in the Spanish motto *Oro y Plata*, which means 'Gold and Silver'.

That of Nebraska represents agriculture, craftsmanship, and commerce by land and sea; the date shown, 'March 1, 1867', is that of the state's admission to the Union, and the motto reads 'Equality before the law'.

The words 'Battle Born' above the white star on the flag of Nevada recall that the Civil War was being waged when the state was admitted to the Union in 1864; the sage-brush below the star is the state flower.

The vessel depicted on the seal and flag of New Hampshire is the *Raleigh*, one of the first ships of the American Navy; the date is that of the Declaration of Independence.

The buff colour of New Jersey's flag is said to be that chosen by George Washington for the emblems of his forces; the ploughs on the coat of arms represent agriculture, and the supporters exemplify the motto 'Liberty and Prosperity'.

A

B

A. Montana
B. Nebraska
C. Nevada
D. New Hampshire
E. New Jersey

C

D

E

New Mexico

New York

North Carolina

North Dakota

Ohio

The emblem on the flag of New Mexico is the Zia sun-symbol of the state's aborigines, the Zuni Indians; the colours red and yellow show that it was formerly ruled by Imperial Spain.

In the coat of arms which appears on the seal and flag of the state of New York the shield depicts a scene on the Hudson River; the supporters represent freedom and justice, and the soaring eagle upon the globe which forms the crest symbolizes the motto *Excelsior*, meaning 'Ever upward, higher'.

The flag of North Carolina suggests the first Confederate flag, the Stars and Bars; the dates of two important declarations of independence are shown in the hoist.

Two national emblems, the thirteen stars and the American Eagle, appear on the flag of North Dakota, which is believed to be derived from the colours of the state militia during the Spanish-American War of 1898.

In its design and colours the tapering burgee which forms the flag of Ohio recalls the Stars and Stripes; the stars indicate that this was the seventeenth state to be admitted to the Union and the circle suggests its colloquial name, the 'Buckeye State'.

The flag of Oklahoma displays two emblems of peace, the olive branch and the American Indian *calumet* or peace-pipe, crossed upon an Indian brave's shield, adorned with seven eagle feathers.

The shield on the obverse of the flag of Oregon displays symbols of the departure of the British as the Americans arrive by land and sea; the reverse of the flag depicts a golden beaver.

Upon the flag of Pennsylvania appear the state's arms; the shield displays emblems of commerce and agriculture, also represented by the supporters — two farm-horses; the scroll bears the motto 'Virtue, Liberty, and Independence'.

As is shown by the thirteen gold stars on its flag, Rhode Island was among the states which formed the Union; the anchor is the time-honoured symbol of hope.

One of the earliest revolutionary flags was that devised in 1776 by Colonel Moultrie: a crescent moon in the upper hoist of a dark blue field. With the addition of a palmetto tree at the centre of the flag, South Carolina adopted the Moultrie flag when it seceded from the Union in 1860.

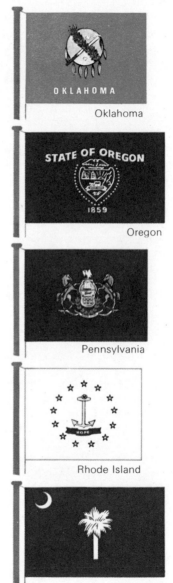

Oklahoma

Oregon

Pennsylvania

Rhode Island

South Carolina

The state seal which appears on the flag of South Dakota bears symbols of agriculture, industry, and commerce; the sun emblem which surrounds it endorses the claim that this is the 'Sunshine State'.

The three white stars on the flag of Tennessee indicate that this was the third state, after the original thirteen, to be admitted to the Union.

After passing from the control of France to that of Spain, Texas was ruled by Mexico; largely colonized by the Americans and English, it at last gained independence. It then adopted the flag which it retained after it was admitted to the Union – a fitting emblem for the 'Lone Star State'.

On the seal and flag of Utah the American Eagle is shown above a symbol of industry, the beehive; the supporters are two American flags, and the dates are important in the history of the state of Utah. In 1847 the first Mormons entered, and settled in, Salt Lake Valley, and in 1896 the state was admitted to the Union.

The landscape depicted on the flag of Vermont includes the 'Liberty Tree' dominating the symbols of agriculture, and the motto is 'Unity and Freedom'.

The seal and flag of Virginia represent the armed figure of Virtue trampling underfoot the emblem of oppression; the Latin motto *Sic Semper Tyrannis* is appropriate: 'Thus ever to tyrants'.

As the state of Washington was named after the hero of America's independence, it seems fitting that his image should be depicted on its seal and flag.

The seal on the flag of West Virginia includes the emblems of freedom and the fight for freedom and figures representing agriculture and mining; the motto *Montani Semper Liberi* makes the proud declaration 'Mountaineers forever free'.

The coat of arms on the flag of Wisconsin includes a shield depicting the implements of agriculture and industry; the supporters are a seaman and a farmer, the crest is a beaver, the historic thirteen stars appear on a scroll, and the motto is 'Forward'.

The state seal of Wyoming appears on the figure of a buffalo silhouetted in white upon a flag of the traditional American colours, red, white, and blue.

South Dakota

Tennessee

Texas

Utah

Vermont

Virginia

Washington

West Virginia

Wisconsin

Wyoming

119

Pan-American Union flag.

CENTRAL AND SOUTH AMERICA

The Caribbean

Where Columbus made his first landfall in the Americas is uncertain – it may have been on Watling Island in the Bahamas. Later he discovered the two largest islands in the Caribbean: Cuba, which he at first mistook for Japan, and Haiti, which, in compliment to the Spanish monarchs who had made his venture possible, he called Hispaniola.

Wherever it was accomplished, his landing was made with great pomp and circumstance; clad in scarlet, he himself bore the royal standard of Spain, quartering the golden castle on red of Castile with the red lion on silver of Leon. His ships' captains, also richly attired, carried a white banner bearing a green cross and the letters 'F' and 'Y', for Fernando and Ysabel.

It seemed appropriate that when, in 1932, the Pan-American Union decided to express in a flag its ideal of achieving solidarity throughout the whole of the New World, this should pay tribute to Columbus's achievement. His flagship, the *Santa Maria*, is represented by a central cross, behind which gleams the traditional 'Bronze sun of the Incas', and his two other vessels, the *Pinta* and the *Niña*, by the two smaller crosses of similar pattern which flank it.

When the Cubans' long struggle for independence from Spain began about 1850, their exiled leader asked a comrade to design a suitable flag. This emblem, *La Estrella Solitaria*,

The first European flags in America. Columbus and his ships' captains go ashore bearing the royal standard of Spain and a flag charged with the initials of their patrons, Fernando and Ysabel.

Cuba: national and merchant flag, and ensign.

Haiti: national flag and ensign.

Dominican Republic: national flag and ensign.

'The Solitary Star', has become the national and merchant flag and ensign of Cuba now that independence has been achieved. It is striped horizontally, three blue and two white stripes, with a red triangle bearing the white star in the hoist. The jack places the white star in a flag divided horizontally; the upper part is red in the hoist, displaying a white star, and white in the fly, and the lower part is blue.

The western part of the island which Columbus called Hispaniola is now known as Haiti. When its Negroes rose in revolt against their white rulers, their leader is said to have ripped the white stripe from the French tricolour, leaving the blue to represent the Negroes and the red the mulattos. The merchant flag of Haiti is now halved vertically, black and red; the national flag and ensign shows at its centre the weapons of war grouped round a palm tree.

The eastern part of the island now forms the Dominican Republic. Its merchant flag is quartered blue and red by a white cross, and the national flag and ensign places the country's arms at the centre of the cross.

Recently some of the West Indian islands within the British Commonwealth have achieved independence, and a number have exchanged badges on the Blue Ensign for their own flags.

On becoming independent within the Commonwealth in 1962, Jamaica adopted a national flag bearing a gold saltire; it is black in the hoist and fly and green at the top and bottom. On the Queen's personal flag for Jamaica, approved in 1966, the royal emblem is centred on a St George's Cross shown with a golden pineapple on each of its arms.

When Jamaica became independent its former dependency, the Cayman Islands, became a British colony and now places its own badge on the Blue Ensign. This includes local emblems such as a turtle and a pineapple plant as well as the Lion of England and the text 'He hath founded it upon the seas'.

The badge of the Leeward Islands, whose design includes a large pineapple, was designed by the group's former Governor, Sir Benjamin Pine! Female figures appear on the badges of the British Virgin Islands and Montserrat. Antigua and St Kitts-Nevis, also within the Leewards, have recently chosen new flags of striking design.

Also achieving their independence in 1962, Trinidad and

Jamaica: national flag.

Antigua: national flag.

St Kitts-Nevis: national flag.

Trinidad and Tobago: national flag.

Barbados: national flag.

Dominica: badge on the British Blue Ensign.

Tobago selected a new national flag with a black stripe, fimbriated with white, crossing a red field from the top of the hoist to the bottom of the fly. On the Queen's personal flag for these islands, approved in 1966, the royal emblem almost obscures a representation of one of Columbus's three ships, white on blue, which appears below two humming-birds, white on black.

Barbados, near the Windward Islands, formerly displayed on its badge a picture of Britannia ruling the waves. Since the island obtained independence within the Commonwealth in 1966, the head of the trident, in black, appears in the centre of its new flag, which bears three vertical stripes, blue, gold, and blue in colour.

The badge of the Windward Islands places a shield, quartered red, yellow, green, and white, within a garter surmounted by the royal crown; the Latin motto *I Pede Fausto* signifies 'Go with a fortunate foot'.

The new badge of Dominica, approved for use on the Blue Ensign in 1965, consists of the island's coat of arms. The shield bears the emblems of a coco-nut palm, a Dominican *crapaud* or edible toad, a carib canoe, and a banana tree; the supporters are two parrots and the crest is the Lion of England. The motto in the local patois *Après Bondie c'est la Terre* means 'After the Good Lord we love the soil'.

Two other islands within the Windward group adopted flags in 1967. That of Grenada is a horizontal tricolour, blue, yellow, and green; a sprig consisting of two leaves and a nutmeg is displayed at the centre. That of St Lucia replaces its former badge – a black shield bearing a device in which two lengths of cane quartered two roses with two *fleurs-de-lis*, representing the claim that the French once made to this island; it is a blue flag bearing a black triangle bordered with white and with a yellow triangle at its base.

The badge of St Vincent, showing two female figures at an altar, with the Latin motto *Pax et Justitia*, 'Peace and Justice',

Grenada: national flag.

St Lucia: national flag.

St Vincent: badge on the British Blue Ensign.

125

Puerto Rico: national flag.

is still in use, but it is proposed to supersede this by a flag resembling that of Grenada with stripes of tartan green, yellow, and blue, and a central device representing a sprig bearing leaves and berries.

Puerto Rico changed hands after the Spanish-American War of 1898, and in 1952 it became a self-governing commonwealth within the United States of America. Its national flag is that borne by the island's patriots when with the Cubans they revolted against Spanish rule; it is identical with the flag of Cuba except that its colours are reversed. The flag of the Governor-General is white, and represents in the hoist the seal granted in 1511 by Ferdinand and Isabella of Spain; its ornate design includes a number of religious symbols.

The flag of the American Virgin Islands is white and bears two United States emblems: the American Eagle and a red, white, and blue shield carrying thirteen stripes. In the hoist and fly respectively there appear the letters 'V' and 'I'.

Though some distance from Jamaica, the Turks and Caicos Islands, like the Cayman Islands, were one of its dependencies, and, again like the Caymans, they became a separate British colony when Jamaica gained independence in 1962. Their former badge, which appeared on the Blue Ensign, depicted a native at work on a beach near some huts, with a three-masted sailing-ship in the offing. Their present badge, which also appears on the Blue Ensign, consists of a gold shield displaying three of the products of this group of islands: a Queen conch shell, a spiny lobster, and a Turk's head cactus.

Separating the Caribbean Sea from the Atlantic is a group

of islands called the Bahamas. Its badge, which appears on the Blue and the Red Ensign, represents a British vessel chasing two pirate ships which are about to disappear over the horizon. This scene is surrounded by a garter emblem bearing the Latin motto *Commercia expulsis piratis restituta*, which can be translated 'Commerce restored by the defeat of the pirates'; the garter is surmounted by a crown, and at the foot of the badge is a scroll bearing the word 'Bahamas'.

Even farther out in the Atlantic, to the north-east of the Caribbean, is the group of islands known as the Bermudas, Shakespeare's 'still-vexed Bermoothes'. Their badge appears on the Red Ensign and consists of a shield on which a lion is shown grasping another more ornate shield which bears a representation of an event important in the islands' colonization: the wreck – in 1609 when the group was still uninhabited – of Admiral Sir George Somers's vessel, the *Sea Venture*, on a reef which is still known as Sea Venture Flat.

Turks and Caicos Islands: former badge on the British Blue Ensign.

Bahamas: badge on the British Blue and Red Ensigns.

Bermuda: badge on the British Red Ensign.

Mexico and Central America

The southern part of the New World was long ruled by Spain, and when the Spanish Empire fell it was divided into a number of independent republics.

Until recently, the merchant flag of Mexico did not bear the national arms, but it has now been brought into line with the national flag and ensign. Hence the Mexican emblem is a vertical tricolour of green, white, and red, bearing its arms at the centre; these are based on the Aztec legend that an eagle standing on a cactus and holding a serpent in its beak would

(Above) Aztec warriors look on as an eagle with a serpent in its beak alights upon a cactus. This was the sign for which the tribe had waited: a city and an empire were born as the prophecy was fulfilled. Tenochtilan was built on this swampy island, and the foundations of modern Mexico were laid.

reveal the place where this wandering people might settle.

The isthmus south of Mexico was for a time united as the Central American Federation, and its five nations still use variants of the Federation's flag, which was striped horizontally, blue, white, and blue.

Guatemala keeps the same colours, but has rearranged them to run vertically. Its merchant flag therefore bears three vertical stripes, blue, white, and blue; as is usual in Latin America, the national flag and ensign places the country's arms on the central stripe.

(Opposite) the national arms on the Mexican tricolour recall the event illustrated above.

(Right) Guatemala: national flag and ensign.

Honduras: national
and merchant flag.

British Honduras: badge
on the British Blue Ensign.

El Salvador: national flag
and ensign.

Honduras still uses the Federation flag, with the addition of a distinguishing emblem. The national and merchant flag bears five blue stars on the white stripe to express the hope that the five republics of central America will again unite. The ensign replaces them with the national arms.

The badge of British Honduras, which appears in the fly of the Blue Ensign, is a shield divided into three sections, displaying the Union Flag, a woodman's implements, and a sailing vessel, the last two to represent the mahogany trade.

Like Honduras, El Salvador uses the flag of the old Federation suitably distinguished. The merchant flag places the words *Dios Union y Libertad*, 'God, Unity, and Freedom', on the central stripe, whereas the national flag and ensign incorporates these words into the arms displayed on that stripe.

The national and merchant flag and ensign of Nicaragua also places the national arms at the centre of a flag striped horizontally, blue, white, and blue, but the flag itself is considerably longer than those of either Honduras or El Salvador.

Costa Rica distinguishes its flags by placing a red stripe at the centre of the flag of the Central American Federation. Its national and merchant flag is striped horizontally, blue, white, red, white, blue; the ensign as usual adds the national arms on the central stripe, but places them towards the hoist.

The Republic of Panama was never within the Central American Federation. Formerly part of Colombia, it became independent only in 1903, and naturally its flag is totally different from any of those which once formed the Federation. Its national and merchant flag and ensign, which is quartered, has red, white, and blue as its colours.

The Panama Canal Zone, through which that waterway runs, is in fact under United States jurisdiction. The shield displayed at the centre of its dark blue flag is red, white, and blue, and includes the traditional thirteen stripes; below these a sailing vessel is shown passing through a narrow stretch of the canal. The motto runs 'The Land Divided, the World United'.

Nicaragua: national and merchant flag, and ensign.

Costa Rica: national and merchant flag.

Panama: national and merchant flag, and ensign.

131

Ecuador: merchant flag.

Colombia: national flag.

Venezuela: national flag and ensign.

South America

The hero of South American independence, Simon Bolivar, aimed not only at freeing the continent from Spanish rule but at uniting it into one great republic. He succeeded only in liberating and uniting a stretch of territory in its north-west, but his Great Colombia Republic soon broke up into three separate nations. These still use the flag one of his followers designed to symbolize 'golden America as separated by the blue sea from the bloodthirsty rule of Spain'.

The merchant flag of Ecuador is a horizontal tricolour, yellow, light blue, and red, with the upper stripe double the width of the other two. The national flag and ensign displays the country's arms in the centre; these include a coastal scene, dominated by Mount Chimborazo, and an off-shore steamer, representing commerce.

The national flag of Colombia is similar to that of Ecuador, except that its central stripe is dark blue. The merchant flag places at its centre a white star surrounded by a red-bordered blue oval; the ensign replaces this by the Colombian arms, which symbolize the Panama isthmus – formerly part of

Colombian territory – separating the Atlantic and Pacific.

The Venezuelan merchant flag has the same colours as the flags of Ecuador, but its horizontal stripes are equal, and at its centre is an arc of seven white stars. The national flag and ensign places the country's arms in the upper hoist: a shield representing agricultural wealth by a wheatsheaf, and the *llanos* (broad plains) by an untamed white horse.

The region to the east of Venezuela was formerly known as British Guiana, and placed on the Blue Ensign a badge showing a three-masted ship with sails set, and a scroll bearing the Latin motto *Damus Petimusque Vicissim*, which could be translated 'We both give and seek'. On becoming independent within the Commonwealth as Guyana, it adopted a flag showing two fimbriated triangles, one yellow and one reddish brown, extending from the hoist of a green flag.

Surinam, Dutch Guinea, flies a white flag on which an oval ring, in black, joins five stars of different colours. The Netherlands Antilles, off the Venezuelan coast, also fly a white flag, on which a blue horizontal stripe bearing six white stars is placed across a red vertical stripe.

(Left) Surinam: national flag.

(Below) Guyana: national flag.

Peru: national flag.

Bolivia: national flag and ensign.

The flag of Peru, so different from the emblems of the countries farther north which had belonged to the Great Colombia Republic, is reputed to have had a romantic origin. When freedom fighters, intent on liberating their country from the Spaniards, landed on its coast, a flock of birds is said to have soared aloft in fright – whereupon their leader, seeing the red and white plumage gleaming in the sun, shouted 'Behold the flag of liberty!'. This inspired the merchant flag of Peru, which is striped vertically, red, white, and red. There are two versions of the Peruvian arms; both include a llama, a tree and a cornucopia to symbolize the country's natural resources. Placed at the centre of the merchant flag, the simpler form of the national arms converts it into the national flag, the more complicated into the ensign.

Bolivia, which at one time was known as Upper Peru, is named after Simon Bolivar. The three horizontal stripes upon its merchant flag, red, gold, and green, are said to represent the country's animal, mineral, and vegetable wealth. The national flag and ensign displays its arms on the central stripe;

these also symbolize the wealth of the country, by a llama, a tree, a wheatsheaf, and a house.

The national and merchant flag and ensign of Chile was designed by an American officer serving with the engineers of the Chilean Army. He was obviously intent upon producing a simplified version of the American flag, reducing its stars and stripes to the bare minimum, and he similarly followed United States practice in using the flag's canton as a jack. One white star also appears on Chile's arms; these are placed on the national flag to form the President's standard.

The red, white, and blue horizontal tricolour of Paraguay, which was adopted by that country when it won its independence from Spain, is distinguished from that of the Netherlands by the badges placed at the centre of the national and merchant flag and ensign. A different emblem appears on each of the flag's two sides: that on the obverse includes a gold star between wreaths of palm and olive, that on the reverse a lion guarding the 'Cap of Liberty', the traditional emblem of a freed slave.

Chile: national and merchant flag, and ensign.

Paraguay: obverse of national and merchant flag, and ensign.

Argentina: national flag and ensign.

Uruguay: national and merchant flag, and ensign.

Although very similar to the flag of the Central American Federation, the emblem of the Argentine Republic is said to have derived its colours from those of the cockade worn by the nationalists during their fight for freedom. The merchant flag of Argentina is striped horizontally, light blue, white, and light blue; the national flag and ensign displays at the centre the 'Sun of May', whose sudden appearance through the clouds was regarded as a good omen for the newly-independent state.

After gaining its freedom from Spanish domination, Uruguay was formed in 1828, through the mediation of Britain, as a 'buffer state' between Brazil and the Argentine Republic. It shows its relationship with Argentina by the 'Sun of May' in the canton and the light blue and white stripes of its national and merchant flag and ensign.

The Falkland Islands, being within the British Commonwealth, place a badge depicting a blue shield within a white circle on the Blue Ensign. On its upper part appears a hornless ram, and below this are the wavy blue and white stripes which form the heraldic symbol for the sea; upon these is shown the vessel *Desire* in which John Davis was sailing when he discovered the Falklands. The motto, 'Desire the Right', is a deliberate pun upon the name of Davis's ship.

While Columbus was discovering the New World on behalf of Spain, Portuguese explorers were rounding the Cape of Good Hope to investigate the lands farther east. Anxious to avoid disputes between the two leading Catholic powers, Pope Alexander VI decreed in 1493 that the meridian 100 leagues west of the Cape Verde Islands should become a frontier; all newly-discovered lands to its east were to go to Portugal, all to its west to Spain. His intention was to assign the regions beyond the Cape to Portugal and all America to Spain, but the demarcation line was altered to 370 leagues in the Spanish-Portuguese treaty of the following year, so that the eastern part of South America was allocated to Portugal.

This included what is now Brazil, which retained the Portuguese language when it gained its independence. Its national and merchant flag and ensign is green, with a gold diamond at its centre; upon this is displayed a celestial globe bearing a number of stars. An equatorial girdle bears the words *Ordem e Progresso*, 'Order and Progress'.

Falkland Islands: badge on the British Blue Ensign.

Brazil: national and merchant flag, and ensign.

AUSTRALASIA

Australia

The national flag of Australia, which has been flown since the beginning of the century, consists of the British Blue Ensign distinguished by a regional emblem. Beneath the Union Flag in the canton appears a large seven-pointed 'Commonwealth Star', and in the fly are five smaller stars, representing the constellation of the Southern Cross. All these stars are white, and similarly placed upon the Red Ensign they form Australia's merchant flag.

The Queen's personal flag for Australia was approved in 1962. It places the royal emblem upon a field displaying the

National flag of Australia.

Personal flag for Australia.

arms of the Commonwealth of Australia, which combine the emblems of its six states.

Having hitherto worn the British White Ensign, the Royal Australian Navy adopted its own White Ensign in 1967. This still bears the Union Flag in the canton, but the St George's Cross has been replaced by stars similar to those on the national flag, except that they are blue on a white field.

The ensigns of the Royal Australian Air Force and the Australian Civil Air Service adapt the symbols on the national flag to correspond to the British ensigns.

White Ensign of the Royal Australian Navy.

Royal Australian Air Force ensign.

Australian Civil Air ensign.

Destruction of the *Emden* by HMAS *Sydney* in World War 1.

Each of the six states which form the Commonwealth of Australia has its own coat of arms, and these emblems, suitably adapted, are displayed in the fly of the British Blue Ensign hoisted over state government buildings.

The badge of Western Australia represents the black swan, which is indigenous to this region, on a yellow circle.

That of South Australia also depicts a native bird, the white-backed piping shrike, again upon a yellow circle.

The badge of Queensland displays the royal crown at the centre of a Maltese cross, shown in blue on a white circle.

New South Wales uses as its badge the St George's Cross, red on a white circle; at its centre appears a lion, and on each of its arms a star, all in gold.

The island of Tasmania also displays the Lion of England, in red, on a white circle.

Victoria, then of course a colony and the first in Australia to have its own warship, HMS *Nelson*, was likewise the first to have its own flag, in 1865; it displayed the Southern Cross in the fly of the Blue Ensign, the royal crown being added about seven years later.

The Southern Cross has been regarded as a suitable emblem for Australia – and for New Zealand – for over a century. According to Frank Cayley's admirable book *Flag of Stars*, a flag somewhat similar to the present badge of New South Wales was suggested in the early 1820s: 'That first "flag of stars" in Australia's history was a white flag charged with the Red Cross of St George, having in each corner a star to symbolize the Southern Hemisphere under the constellation of the Southern Cross.'.

Though this flag was never popular, it influenced several later designs, including ensigns on which the British Union Flag was placed in the canton of a variety of fields: the St George's Cross bearing five stars on its arms and centre, and a number of horizontal blue and white stripes symbolizing the oceans between Australia and Great Britain; a white field bearing a blue cross of the St George type, with the usual five white stars; and a leaping kangaroo!

As a result of a public competition held in 1901, the present Southern Cross design was chosen and this was approved by Edward VII in 1903 as the flag of Australia.

Western Australia

South Australia

Queensland

New South Wales

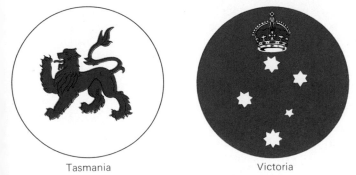

Tasmania

Victoria

Each state in the Commonwealth of Australia has a badge adapted from the state arms; these are placed in the fly of the British Blue Ensign, which is flown over state government buildings.

National flag of New Zealand.

United Tribes of
New Zealand flag.

White Ensign of the Royal New
Zealand Navy.

New Zealand

The national flag of New Zealand, like that of Australia, places
the Southern Cross emblem in the fly of the British Blue Ensign,
but represents it differently: only four stars are shown instead
of five, and they are not white but red with a white fimbriation.
The four stars are also shown on the merchant flag, but here
they are depicted in white on the British Red Ensign.

The Queen's personal flag for New Zealand, like that for
Australia, was authorized in 1962, and places Her Majesty's
emblem on a field formed by New Zealand's arms. They combine the Southern Cross with symbols of the nation's commerce
and of its animal, vegetable, and mineral wealth: two heraldic
ships, a fleece, a wheatsheaf, and mining tools.

In 1968 the Royal New Zealand Navy, which had previously
worn the British White Ensign, replaced this by its own White
Ensign, with the Union Flag in the canton and the Southern
Cross, represented by four red stars, in the fly; the jack is
formed by the New Zealand national flag. The ensign of the

Royal New Zealand Air Force places the letters 'NZ' in white at the centre of a target similar to that on the British Royal Air Force ensign; the New Zealand Civil Air ensign places the stars of the Southern Cross in the fourth quarter of the corresponding British ensign.

According to Frank Cayley's *Flag of Stars*, the present New Zealand flag had several unofficial forerunners. The necessity for such a flag was made clear when in 1830 a New Zealand vessel was seized by the customs authorities at Sydney for not flying any flag! As the region had not yet become a colony, ships built in its yards could not sail under British register.

A few years later the newly-appointed British Resident in New Zealand asked the authorities in Sydney to design a suitable flag. However the result – four horizontal blue stripes on a white field, with the Union Jack in the canton – disappointed him for it contained so little of the colour red which the Maoris associate with rank.

He therefore had three designs voted for by the white settlers and the Maoris. The one chosen was a St George's Cross having

The field of Elizabeth II's personal flag for New Zealand *(left)* shows emblems of the country's wealth and commerce, as well as the Southern Cross.

(Below, left) Royal New Zealand Air Force ensign.

(Below, right) Royal New Zealand Civil Air ensign.

143

The Western Pacific High Commissioner's emblem is centred on the British Union Flag.

These arms, in the fly of the British Blue Ensign, represent the British Solomon Islands.

The New Hebrides place their badge in the fly of the British Blue Ensign.

in the canton a smaller red cross fimbriated with white on a blue field, with a white star in each quarter.

This flag of the United Tribes of New Zealand was flown for only a few years. Then it was replaced by the British Union Flag and became the house flag of Shaw Savill and Albion Company Limited. For a time the Union Flag was superseded by the British Blue Ensign with the letters 'NZ' in the fly, and the present flag was approved in 1902.

The Pacific

A number of islands and archipelagos in the Pacific Ocean – including the British Solomon Islands, the Gilbert and Ellice Islands, the New Hebrides, and the Phoenix Islands – come under the jurisdiction of the Western Pacific High Commissioner. His emblem is the British Union Flag, bearing at its centre a white circle on which the letters 'WPHC' appear, ensigned with the royal crown and surrounded by a garland. Some of these groups of islands, however, also have their own flags.

The British Solomon Islands Protectorate, for example, puts its arms in the fly of the Blue Ensign. They take the

Guam: Governor's flag.

form of a shield, on whose upper part the Lion of England appears, gold on red, and whose lower part depicts an eagle, a turtle, native weapons, and two frigate birds, on a field quartered blue and white.

The New Hebrides, a group of islands in the southern Pacific, form a condominium, administered jointly by Britain and France. Their badge, flown within a garland at the centre of the British Union Flag and without a garland on the Blue Ensign, shows on a white disc a royal crown with the words 'New Hebrides' in black.

Papua and New Guinea, being administered by the Australian government, use the Blue and Red Ensigns with the Commonwealth Star and the Southern Cross that form the national and merchant flags of Australia.

The island of Guam was formerly Spanish, but towards the end of the nineteenth century it was ceded to the United States, by whom it is used as an air and naval outpost. The seal of the Governor of Guam appears at the centre of a blue flag; it depicts an island scene, including an outrigger canoe.

Nauru, a small island annexed by the Germans in 1888, was taken over by Australia in 1914, and except for a period during the Second World War was administered by that country under a League of Nations mandate and later under a United Nations trusteeship agreement. In 1968 it became independent and now has its own flag. The blue field represents the Pacific Ocean and the sky; the gold horizontal stripe and the white star symbolize Nauru's position immediately south of the Equator.

The Tongan or Friendly Islands form a monarchy within the Commonwealth. The King of Tonga's standard is quartered and displays three stars, a crown, a dove bearing an olive branch in its beak, and three piled swords; at its centre a red Greek cross appears on a white star. The red cross also appears in the white canton of the red Tongan state flag.

The Fiji Islands place their full coat of arms on the Blue Ensign. A lion holding a coco-nut in its paws is shown, gold on red, in the upper part of the shield; the lower part is quartered by a St George's Cross and displays three sugar-canes, a coco-nut palm, a dove carrying an olive branch in its beak, and a bunch of bananas; the supporters are Fijians, and the crest is a Fijian canoe. The motto *Rere Vaka na kalou ka doka na tui* means 'Fear God and honour the king'.

The badge of the Gilbert and Ellice Islands depicts the sun rising over the sea, above which a frigate bird is flying; it is placed on the Blue Ensign.

Samoa, called by the French Navigators' Islands, consists of two groups of islands and islets. Those of Western Samoa were for a time under German rule, but were taken over in 1914 by a New Zealand expeditionary force, and remained under that country's rule until 1962, when they became the

Tonga: royal standard.

Tonga: state flag.

Western Samoa: national and merchant flag.

Gilbert and Ellice Islands: badge on the British Blue Ensign.

Former badge of Western Samoa, replaced by the flag opposite.

first independent Polynesian state. Formerly represented by a badge on the British Blue Ensign showing a beach scene including three coco-nut palms, Western Samoa now has its own national and merchant flag – red, except for a blue canton, upon which the Southern Cross appears as five white stars.

The flag of American Samoa is blue, with a white red-bordered triangle extending from the fly to the hoist. Upon the triangle is shown a flying eagle in natural colours, holding in its talons Samoan emblems denoting wisdom and power.

Some conclusions

Thus the smallest and most remote islands of the southern seas, like the great land-masses of the north, represent their national identity and ideals by the time-honoured method of flying a flag bearing emblems of local significance.

Throughout the world the history of the various regions is symbolized by their flags. A brief comparison with flag books published earlier this century shows how greatly conditions have altered in a lifetime. Gone are many of the ensigns which distinguished colonies in the British Empire; gone too are flags implying French, Belgian, or Dutch rule. They have been replaced by emblems showing that these countries, although perhaps still associated with their former rulers, are now independent sovereign states. There are also two regions whose history and use of flags has only recently begun and no modern flag book would be complete without some mention of Antarctica and space.

The coat of arms assigned to the British Antarctic Territory.

ANTARCTICA

A number of explorers have flown their national flags over the Antarctic, and the Stars and Stripes and United Nations flag were hoisted over the Amundsen-Scott South Pole Station to inaugurate the International Geophysical Year (1957-8).

In 1962 a separate colony, the British Antarctic Territory, was formed from the South Shetlands, South Orkneys, and Graham Land. It was given the arms of the former Falkland Island dependencies. On a white shield are wavy blue lines, to represent snowfields and the Antarctic Ocean, and a gold torch, the symbol of knowledge, on a red triangle. The supporters suggest Britain and Antarctica, a lion and an emperor penguin; the motto is 'Research and Discovery', and the crest displays an explorer's vessel.

In 1965 the Australian National Antarctic Research Expedition adopted a new pendant, to be flown alongside the Australian national flag at all Australian bases in the Antarctic. On a tartan green field a leopard seal, in gold, is outlined in black, and below this the letters 'ANARE' appear above a golden boomerang.

FLAGS IN SPACE

Flags have now been taken not only to the ends of the earth but out into space.

The Russian spacecraft *Luna 1*, which in January 1959 attempted to reach the moon, carried a metal 'pendant' engraved with the name of the Soviet Union. *Luna 2*, which reached the moon on 13 September 1959, scattered over its surface a number of tiny Russian flags.

Luna 9, which landed on the moon in February 1966, carried a pendant bearing the words 'Union of the Soviet Socialist Republics' in the Cyrillic alphabet as well as symbols of the earth, the moon, and the spacecraft's path.

The American astronauts who 'walked in space' displayed their country's flag on the sleeve of their spacesuits and released a larger flag beyond the atmosphere. The American flag was also sent to the moon in June 1966 sealed inside the tubing of the space capsule, *Surveyor 1*.

On 21 July 1969 the Stars and Stripes, wired to stand out firmly in the absence of wind, was planted on the moon by astronauts Neil A. Armstrong and Edwin E. Aldrin.

A flag was raised on the moon for the first time on 21 July 1969.

SIGNAL FLAGS

Signals have been given from time immemorial, but not perhaps very systematically; Greek and Roman literature refers only to the raising or waving of a brightly-coloured cloak. The earliest code of naval signals appears to have been drawn up in the ninth century by the Byzantine Emperor Leo V, but such systems were used solely in the Mediterranean. For a long time only two signals were used by the British Navy: to call the ships' captains into council and warn 'Enemy in sight'.

Not until the seventeenth century was a code of flag-signals employed by the British Navy, but once introduced it developed rapidly, the number of flags and of possible signals being increased and the code becoming more complicated.

Towards the end of the eighteenth century a method invented by a French officer was adopted by the British Royal Navy, and a number of improvements were devised. Each flag was assigned a number, and each hoist of one, two, or three flags had a special meaning; a hoist of flags 2, 9, and 1, for

Flags and pennants of the Revised International Code of Signals.

example, meant 'Engage the enemy as close as possible'.

However this numerary method proved insufficient, and it was clear that something more flexible was needed. In 1800, adapting a suggestion made by an officer of the East India Company's fleet, Sir Home Popham devised what he called his *Telegraphic Signals* or *Marine Vocabulary*, in which each of the hoists of flags meant not a sentence but a word or even a letter. It included ten flags numbered '1' to '9' and '0'; a 'substitute' flag to repeat one already included in a hoist; and a 'telegraph' flag to show that the vocabulary, and not the older numerary system, was being used.

It was in a development of this code that Nelson gave his famous signal at Trafalgar, his hoists being: the telegraph flag; 253; 269; 863; 261; 471; 958; 220, literally 2, substitute, 0; 370; and 4, 21, 19, 24 – the word 'duty', not being included in the vocabulary, had to be spelled out.

In 1804 Sir Home Popham, at the request of the East India Company, adapted his system to meet their needs by compiling a system of *Commercial and Military Signals*. It dealt chiefly with the requirements of ships sailing in convoy.

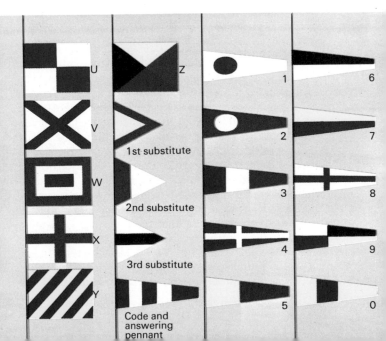

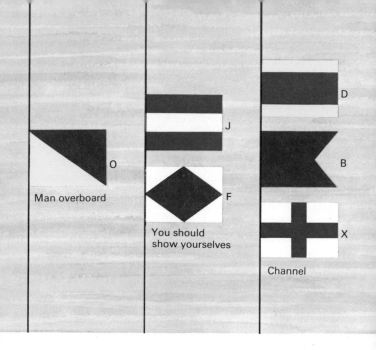

Some examples of signalling using the International Code.

After peace had been restored, Captain Frederick Marryat drew up, in 1817, a code for commercial use combining some of the features of the numerary and vocabulary methods. Successful in itself, it also formed a basis for the later codes.

In 1855 a committee appointed by the British Board of Trade reported that such codes were insufficient: ten flags, even with three 'repeaters', using not more than four flags in one hoist, could provide only 9999 different signals. Instead of ten numerary flags, the *Commercial Code of Signals for the Use of All Nations*, which the committee published in 1857, used eighteen flags, each known not by a number but by a letter. Only the consonants were used, however, for to include the vowels could involve the risk that the four flags of a hoist might spell out some 'objectionable words'.

Though this code made nearly 80,000 different hoists possible, it was found to be inadequate, and in 1899 another Board of Trade committee produced the First International

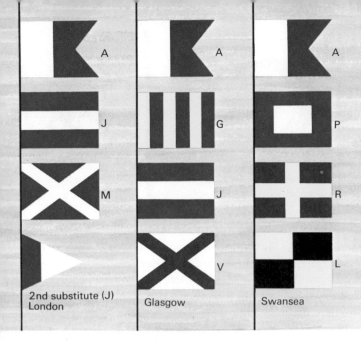

2nd substitute (J)
London

Glasgow

Swansea

Code of Signals. This provided a flag for every letter of the alphabet, any hoists which might spell obscenities being avoided; thus over 375,000 different signals could be made.

Even this code proved unsatisfactory, however, and in 1927 an International Radio Telegraph Conference decided to leave its revision to Great Britain, assisted by representatives of several other governments. The revised International Code includes not only the twenty-six flags and the 'code and answering pennant' but ten numeral flags, ten numbered pennants, and three substitutes, triangular flags for repeating letters or figures.

The British Naval Code, which harmonizes with that of the other member-states of the North Atlantic Treaty Organization, is even more complicated. To the twenty-six alphabetical flags, the ten numeral flags, the ten numbered pennants, the three substitutes, and the code and answering pennant of the International Code it adds a fourth substitute, nine special flags and eleven special pennants, thus enabling an incredible variety of signals to be made.

The crescent moon is the Moslem symbol for the Red Cross.

Only Iran uses this emblem for the Red Cross organization.

INTERNATIONAL FLAGS

Unlike those of ancient Greece, the modern Olympic Games are international. It was not until they were resumed after the Second World War that their flag was hoisted. It displays, on a white field, the symbol of unity, a chain. The colours of its links were probably chosen because they are those most frequently used on the world's flags (page 56).

In 1859 Jean Henri Dunant, a Swiss, was so horrified at the wounds inflicted at the Battle of Solferino that he urged the formation of organized bodies to aid the wounded in wartime. Through his work the first Geneva Convention in 1864 agreed that the wounded and the medical services should be given neutrality. Dunant had also argued that the medical services should have their own flag, and the conference adopted the Swiss flag with colours reversed as the Red Cross emblem (page 89). In Moslem countries, where the cross is identified as a Christian symbol, the red crescent takes its place, though in Iran the device is the lion and sun, also in red. Different as they are, these flags are one in their aim: to symbolize the relief of suffering everywhere, in war and in peace.

Consisting of representatives from almost every state, the United Nations Organization was formed in 1945. Its flag bears a map of the world, white on blue; this centres the continents, seas, and North Pole on the Greenwich meridian; on each side appears an emblem of peace, the olive branch.

The flags of the United Nations and some of its member-states.

BOOKS TO READ

Boutell's Heraldry revised by C. W. Scott-Giles and J. P. Brooke-Little. Frederick Warne, London, 1966.

British Flags by W. G. Perrin. Cambridge Naval and Military Series, Cambridge University Press, London, 1922.

Colours and Standards in the Royal Air Force, published by Her Majesty's Stationery Office, 1957.

Flags for Ship Modellers and Marine Artists by A. A. Purves. Percival Marshall, London, 1950.

Flags of All Nations and its periodical supplements, published by Her Majesty's Stationery Office.

Flag of Stars by F. Cayley. Rigby, Melbourne, 1966.

Flags of the World revised by Capt. E. M. C. Barraclough. Frederick Warne, London, 1969.

Flags over South Africa by R. Gerard. Pretoria Technical College, Pretoria, 1952.

History of the United States Flag by M. M. Quaife. Harper & Row, New York, 1961.

Observer's Book of Flags by I. O. Evans. Observer Pocket Series, Frederick Warne, London, 1959.

Sea Flags: Their General Use by Comdr. H. P. Mead. Brown, Son & Ferguson, Glasgow, 1938.

Standards, Guidons and Colours of the Commonwealth Forces by Major T. J. Edwards. Gale & Polden, Aldershot, 1953.

The Book of Flags by Admiral G. Campbell and I. O. Evans. Sixth edition, Oxford University Press, London, 1969.

Yacht Flags and Ensigns by Capt. E. M. C. Barraclough. Iliffe Books, London, 1951.

INDEX

Page numbers in bold type refer to illustrations.

SOME OTHER TITLES IN THIS SERIES

 Natural History

The Animal Kingdom	Life in the Sea
Australian Animals	Mammals of the World
Bird Behaviour	Natural History Collecting
Birds of Prey	The Plant Kingdom
Fishes of the World	Prehistoric Animals
Fossil Man	Snakes of the World
A Guide to the Seashore	Wild Cats

 Gardening

Chrysanthemums	Garden Shrubs
Garden Flowers	Roses

 Popular Science

Atomic Energy	Mathematics
Computers at Work	Microscopes & Microscopic Life
Electronics	The Weather Guide

Arts

Architecture	Porcelain
Jewellery	Victoriana

General Information

Military Uniforms	Sailing Ships & Sailing Craft
Rockets & Missiles	Sea Fishing
Sailing	Trains

 Domestic Animals & Pets

Budgerigars	Horses & Ponies
Cats	Pets for Children
Dogs	

Domestic Science

Flower Arranging

 History & Mythology

Discovery of	Myths & Legends of
Africa	Ancient Egypt
The American West	Ancient Greece
Japan	The South Seas
North America	